The Dead Philosophers' Café

The Dead Philosophers' Café

*An Exchange of Letters
for Children and Adults*

Nora K. and Vittorio Hösle

Translated by Steven Rendall

UNIVERSITY OF NOTRE DAME PRESS
Notre Dame, Indiana

Translated by Steven Rendall from the German *Das Café der toten Philosophen:
Ein philosophischer Briefwechsel für Kinder und Erwachsene*, by Nora K. and
Vittorio Hösle, published by C. H. Beck'sche Verlagsbuchhandlung

Library of Congress Cataloging-in-Publication Data
K., Nora.
  [Café der Toten Philosophen. English]
  The Dead Philosophers' Café : an exchange of letters for children
and adults / Nora K. and Vittorio Hösle ; translated by Steven Rendall.
     p. cm.
  Includes index.
  Summary: A series of letters between a professor of philosophy and
an eleven-year-old girl.
  ISBN 978-0-268-00894-9 (cloth)
    1. Children and philosophy. [1. Philosophy.   2. Letters.]   I. Hösle,
Vittorio, 1960– .   II. Title.
  B105.C45 K1513   2000
  108'.3—dc21
                                                        99-088246

Contents

Preface

This is how letters in this book came to be written. Nora had long been interested in philosophical questions. On her eleventh birthday she received a copy of Jostein Gaarder's *Sophie's World*. She read the book with great interest, and it aroused her curiosity about a number of issues. When I came to visit, she asked me several questions about philosophy, because she knew I taught the subject. Thus, before we began our correspondence, she asked me once whether the Platonic idea of dinosaurs had died out along with the last individuals of the species—a question that is not without a certain originality. I tried to explain why the idea of dinosaurs would not be affected by the extinction of the individuals; she found my explanation satisfactory, and this led us to adopt the nicknames "Dino-Nora" and "Idea of Dinosaurs." In recognition of the significance of her question I sent her a marzipan dinosaur for Christmas. Our exchange of letters begins with her thank-you note.

Dear Vittorio,

Thanks so much for the marzipan dinosaur! I loved it, and put it on my night-table. That way I can look at it whenever I want to.

Unfortunately, so far I've been able to read only the first page of your book, but soon I'll finish my other book and then I'll begin yours.

In my book on philosophy I am now reading about the Middle Ages. This part is also very exciting. In history, we are still dealing with the Greek notion of women. Aristotle's interpretation made me really mad.

Yours, Nora

Essen, 27 January 1994

Dear Nora,

Thanks for your very nice card, which I was delighted to receive. You are very self-disciplined not to have eaten your marzipan dinosaur immediately—it is only an imitation, not eternal, like an idea . . .

Your criticism of Aristotle put me to a lot of work. Because I think highly of him as well as of you, my feelings were all confused. So yesterday, late in the evening, I walked through Rüttenscheid until I came to a side street I'd never noticed before, in which there was a café. It was called "Café of the Dead but Ever Young Philosophers," and since the name amused me, I went in. I thought it would be completely empty, because who goes to cafés with such funny names? But I was surprised to discover that it was pretty full—though almost everyone there was a man.

I sat down at a table where an old gentleman was already sitting alone (there weren't any more free tables). I nodded to him; to tell the truth, like the other men in the café he struck me as vaguely familiar, though I couldn't put a name to his face. The man opposite me had a short beard, strong lips, and very protuberant forehead. He was stylishly dressed, but his eyes didn't seem to belong to our time.

Bewildered, I stared at him somewhat rudely, and finally asked: "Pardon me, I know I've met you somewhere, but I can't remember your name. Mine's Hösle."

"Aristotle, nice to see you," he distractedly replied.

You won't be surprised to learn that I was surprised—I would never have considered such a thing possible if I hadn't already gotten used to the fact that in philosophy everything is possible. And now I recognized the other men, too: at the billiard table a little man who was obviously Kant was discussing the ontological proof with a dignified-looking bishop, whom he constantly addressed as "dear Anselm," while a rather dandyish, shy young man in a top hat was trying to explain, to a carefully groomed gentleman who kept his eyes fixed on the floor, that subjectivity was the Truth and that the leap of faith went beyond reason.

But naturally I was particularly happy that I was sitting at a table with Aristotle. "Now, listen," I said to him, "I've learned a great deal from you, and I find your works really fantastic, but I know a young lady who is outraged by your notion of women."

"You wouldn't by chance be referring to Dinosaur-Nora?"

"Yes—do you know her too?"

"No, not personally, but good arguments are highly valued in this café, and they always reach us fairly fast. I, too, found it difficult to abandon the belief that species were fixed, but since the extinction of species offered a good argument against my teacher Plato, I am on good terms with Darwin again. Nora caused a new coalition to be formed in our café."

"But then you really have a duty to offer her an apology for your view of women," I said.

"Okay, okay," he said, "gladly. Consider it done. But tell her three things. First, I did not deny, as many people claim, that women have souls—I attribute souls even to plants. Second, we are all children of our times—what I said about slavery is even more embarrassing to me. But if one grows up in a society in which slavery is taken for granted and regarded as natural, and in which women don't study or worry about the idea of dinosaurs, then such views are almost inevitable. And third, I want to point out to you and to Dinosaur Nora that you also hold opinions that will make you blush with shame in a few hundred years. So don't be hard on an old Greek!"

"But I assure you," I said, "that we hold you and your teacher Plato in the highest regard" (unfortunately, I noticed too late that this annoyed him a little). "With your permission," I went on, "I'll write to Nora right after our conversation."

On my way out, however, I met another man, who winked at me and said: "Anyway, Nora is very critical and won't believe what you plan to write to her. So just ask her this: 'If you think that I dreamed all this, can you really distinguish between reality and dream?' And if she says: 'God is not a deceiver,' then you answer: 'Sometimes he deceives us regarding the truth.'"

"Thanks a lot, René; I'll put that at the end of my letter."

And so there you are, with best wishes for today,

Yours, Vittorio

---

30 January 1994

Dear Vittorio,

Many, many thanks for your interesting letter! Now I understand Aristotle's notion of women better. I accept his apology. You can tell him so if you go back to the "Café of the Dead but Ever Young Philosophers." But then please tell him too that although his statement that he lived in an earlier time is correct, he could have taken Plato as a model, because Plato had a basically positive notion of women. Does Aristotle know Diotima? It was she who helped Socrates achieve an important philosophical insight. A woman!

Too bad Plato wasn't there when you visited the café. You would have liked to talk with him, wouldn't you? He must surely have a gentler face than Aristotle does. Oh, yes—don't forget to tell René that I understood something of his question about dream and reality, and this is what I think about it:

Dream and reality are two different worlds. Dream is the world of imagination and thoughts, and from these two something is brewed up that comes from deep inside us. For us, reality is the world of the senses. But it's also the sciences or history or languages. However, do we really experience all of reality? We know almost nothing about God. But all the same He exists. So our reality is not complete, and neither are dreams. Dreams only give us something approximate. You can sometimes learn something from dreams, and also from reality. Maybe both these worlds prepare us for the coming but not yet known world?

I did not wholly understand what René meant when he said: "Sometimes God deceives us about reality."

You know, some day, when I am all grown up, I might go to that café sometime. (When I am mature enough.) Once I was walking through a park and saw a man coming toward me. Because I wanted to rest a little, I sat down on a nearby bench. The man seemed to have the same idea, because he sat down next to me. After a little while he began a conversation with me. It was about this and that. But especially it was about having an "idea." That interested me a lot. Unfortunately, after half an hour he had to go—he said he had an appointment in the Café of the Dead but Ever Young Philosophers. I did not know about this café (I hadn't yet received your letter). So I asked him: "But tell me, where is this strange café? I've never heard its name before!"

He replied: "I mustn't tell you the address yet; if you want to go there you'll have to find it yourself. I hope you succeed! Maybe we'll see each other again there!" Then he walked swiftly away, without even saying "Good-bye."

Today I think I met Plato. Who knows, maybe sometime I'll come with you to the Café of the Dead but Ever Young Philosophers.

Best wishes, hope to see you soon,
Yours, Nora

P.S. On the first page I tried to draw a picture showing how the dream world and the real world are (I know it's obviously not exact).

Essen, 3 February 1994
Dear Nora,

Your letter was loudly applauded in the café. Even Aristotle thought his view of women had been definitively corrected—not to mention his view of children. For after all, you are still a child, and the very fact that you already think so well shows that philosophy is not something exclusively for grownups. A man who seemed very vulnerable and a bit too eccentric for my taste, but all the same extremely sensitive, easily moved to tears, even cried out: "You're amazed that children philosophize *too*? In reality, children are the only ones who can really philosophize. And do you know why? Dinosaur Nora hinted at it in her beautiful picture. First of all, I find it marvelous that she has substituted the forest for our café in this awful urban Rüttenscheid—back to nature, she seems to say, and so do I. Isn't she clever?"

Frankly, I was rather annoyed by this claim. Not because he said that you were clever, but because he thought you were clever *because* you think the same way he does. What would he have said if your opinion differed from his? These philosophers can be vain and opinionated too! But I saw that this man was very narcissistic as soon as I looked at his face—he didn't have any of Aristotle's sharp and sober features.

"Second," he went on, "she wrote that we are crossing a river and have to paddle hard against the current in order to arrive at philosophy. What, then, is this river that separates the place where we live (ahem, I mean the place where other people live and where we once lived) from philosophy? It is life with all its swirling and often its shallows. And the older we get, the more this river of life grows, and it becomes ever more difficult to cross. However, at its source, to which Nora is still relatively close, you can still jump over it with ease; you don't need a boat at all. Therefore it is only in childhood that one can truly philosophize. —Ah! If only I hadn't sent my children to the orphanage! Then I would have become a better philosopher, because they would have inspired me." (Again, this narcissistic way of relating everything to himself!)

There was a long silence after this passionate outburst on the part of the sensitive lover of children. But then an old man stood up; he had long white hair, eyes deep-sunk under his forehead, and a large, hooked nose:

"As always, Jean-Jacques, you exaggerate, although you draw attention to something important and often neglected. Perhaps you will make Nora like you, but in reality she can hardly want you to be right. For the poor child cannot remain a child; she has to grow old like everyone else, except for us, since we are dead but enjoy eternal youth all the same. For it would be terrible if she now had the feeling that life could no longer give her anything new. But we can agree on at least one thing: the river in fact grows broader and therefore more difficult to cross. Of course, our strength also increases, and our hope is that our muscles grow even faster than the power of the water. To be sure, that is not the case for everyone, perhaps only for a few. For the others, it is probably true that in the course of their lives they move farther and farther from philosophy, though in their childhoods they were not so far from it. However, ladies and gentlemen, that cannot be so in general; otherwise we would all have to be children, whereas we are only eternally young. Indeed, there is not a single child among us, and if truth be told, we don't really hope that Nora meets us any-time soon."

"God spare us that!" said a beautiful, spiritual-looking woman. "And even as a visitor she cannot visit us soon, but must still write many letters. For what we most passionately desire we cannot quickly acquire, since otherwise we would be unhappy, like most people out there, and perhaps even more unhappy than those who don't have what they desire—since they at least still have their longing."

"Diotima!" I shouted, "at last I have met you in person! Now I no longer doubt whether you really exist. Macho men still maintain that although you may have been the most important woman philosopher, it was a man who invented you. Now I can see you with my own eyes, and I am convinced of your reality."

"You poor man," she replied, "you have to see in order to be convinced. Didn't you understand Nora's letter? Did you understand René's remark even less than she did? At least she was asking what he meant by it, and thus at least she knows that she knows nothing. You poor devil, you're even more ignorant than she is. If God can betray us regarding the truth, that is, if He can deceive us concerning the facts of the world of the senses in order to force us to penetrate to deeper truths, why should Plato have not simply invented me in order to show that women can also philosophize? Something invented still exists, for there are people who think about it; in any case it is not nothing."

My head was spinning, and I excitedly looked around the room, searching for Plato, who I hoped could solve the riddle. But Diotima seemed to have understood what I was thinking:

"We haven't made things so easy that you can simply ask Plato. In any case, he is seldom here; he has a tendency to make himself scarce and to hang out in parks and suchlike. I am giving you a tip: ask Nora to explain to you what he told her about the idea. In particular, you should ask her opinion about whether the idea of the dinosaur would still exist if not only all dinosaurs, but also all men that could conceive of dinosaurs, were extinct. That is a difficult question, to be sure, but you won't get an answer to it from me, for people only understand what they have discovered for themselves. I am only the midwife of knowledge, not its mother."

On one hand, I was confused and also somewhat disappointed by this conversation, yet on the other, it means that I can look forward to your next letter!

Yours, Vittorio

Dear Vittorio,

Thanks for your letter, I was very happy to get it. I'm pleased that my first letter aroused so much discussion in the café. —Unfortunately, my parents have forbidden me to hang out in parks. Therefore I've not seen Plato again.

But I still know (or at least I think I know) what he said the first time I saw him: "Did you ever have an idea you thought of yourself?"

I reflected for a minute and then replied: "Yes, once in religion class we dealt with allegories. The homework was to invent our own allegory. I did that."

"An allegory! Allegories are very, very important," he murmured, "I myself like to use allegories, because they make it possible to understand ideas better! For example, when you compare human beings with the shadows the light outside throws against the wall of a cave."

"What?" Outraged, I jumped to my feet. "Us, shadows? We're the highest creatures on earth. We are not shadows!"

"Just because we are creatures, we are a kind of shadow. The word 'creature' comes from the Latin verb *creare,* to create. We are created. That means that someone (?) had the *idea* of *creating* us. Do you understand?"

"Well, that is really very complicated," I admitted. Then he asked me: "Why do you think we are the highest creatures on earth?"

I had to mull that over. "I think because we have a soul that God can recognize."

"Precisely! We human beings are divided into two parts, so to speak. One half is spiritual: we can (as you already said) recognize God, feel happiness, etc. The other half is our body, which lives in the world of the senses. Both of them derive from an idea: our body for living is an idea. The second idea is God's breath. He has given us part of His spirit. He did that so we could (sometime) come to know the world. Animals don't have this spirit. Neither do plants. Nevertheless, your idea is important, very important. Why, you will learn in biology and chemistry."

"But what does that have to do with shadows?" I asked impatiently.

"We are the shadows of this idea of the two-part creature. Because God has our idea, we can live. We are imitations of the idea 'human being.' Every kind of living being, and even beings that are not alive, such as stones, have an idea."

"So when I have an idea, it's not my idea at all, but already existed?" I asked excitedly.

"That is a difficult question. Unfortunately, I don't have time to explain it to you just now. But you can ask my friend Vittorio. Maybe he can explain it to you."

Then he went away. My question has remained unanswered. Can you answer it for me?

Now, about Dinos. I think the idea of the dinosaur will continue to exist when we human beings are extinct. Only there won't be any creature left that could recognize them. Animals and plants don't know things. No spirit was given them. But there are nonetheless still discoveries like bones that point to an idea. It's just that for the moment the idea of a dinosaur doesn't have a place on earth.

Anyway, you can tell Diotima that I believe that she exists as well. She is ultimately also an idea. Whether God's or Plato's, I don't know. There are lots of things we can't see that are still there.

What kind of lover of children is it who puts his kids in an orphanage? Jean-Jacques is going to have to make up for that.

Oh yes—are there any natural philosophers like Heraclitus or Anaximander in the café?

Do you know what philosopher I find very nice? Augustine.

Hope to hear from you soon,
Yours, Nora

P.S. Could you please write a little more clearly in your next letter? I can hardly read your writing.

Essen, 15 February 1994

Dear Nora,

When I went into the café, René immediately came up to me and asked: "Anything new from Nora?" Then he led me over to a little table. I gave him your letter, which he read through very carefully. When he came to your remark about the lover of children who put his own children in an orphanage, he smiled a little maliciously. "We'd better not show this to Jean-Jacques," he said, "otherwise he'll start crying or have an attack of hysteria. How much Nora knows! The story was made famous by that old man over there" (here he threw a glance—it's impolite to point at people with one's finger!—in the direction of a gray-haired man with a wrinkled face who was looking around mockingly), "and now even children know it. It's true, my good man; philosophers don't always live according to the principles they teach. That man over there with the big eyes and the huge nose once put it this way: 'Those who show the way don't follow it themselves.' It may even be that people become ethicists in order to compensate for their own moral shortcomings, and that a new theoretical sensitivity to children is developed in order to redeem an injustice committed against one's own children. But if that were always the case (Nora needn't worry: it is *not* always the case!), then our club would be a public menace.

"It is not without jealousy that I note that Nora is particularly interested in Plato. You don't have to look around—he's not here today, either. So stop glancing this way and that, I'm not an evil spirit deceiving you in some way. Plato makes himself scarce. Maybe he's roaming through the Revier Park looking for Nora. Poor Plato, he isn't aware of Nora's parents' strict prohibition. But of course her parents are also making a mistake: anything forbidden becomes particularly attractive. So they are driving their child straight into Plato's arms. Could that be exactly what they're trying to do? Might they be so crafty that they forbid, hoping she will do just what they've forbidden, that she will go on philosophizing as much as she is able? How hard it is to know the human heart! So—now we've finally arrived at our subject. It seems to me that one can use the word 'idea' in very different ways. For me, ideas are something that occur in our consciousness, and our consciousness is different from the material world. The former I called *res cogitans,* and the latter *res extensa.* Today I might use other terms, because it is perhaps not very appropriate to call consciousness a 'thing.' But in any case, feelings, thoughts, and even pains are something quite different from physical, corporeal objects that I can measure."

"Wait a minute," I said, "pains are something physical. I mean, not all pains, for example, not a bad conscience, but pains like toothaches."

Descartes looked at me for a long time, then laughed in a supercilious way. "Yes, people thought that for a long time, one could even say, until I came along. I point out that toothaches belong to the world of consciousness. The tooth itself and the inflammation of the nerve— that's all physical. But the fact that the inflammation also causes *pain*—that's something else. An unconscious person's tooth can be inflamed without causing any pain. And vice versa: do you know what phantom pains are?"

"Not exactly."

"Well, there are people who have had to have a leg amputated (for example, if they have smoked too much). What's incredible is that such a person often has terrible pains in the right foot—even when that foot no longer exists! Thus foot-pain belongs to the world of consciousness."

"I perceive my consciousness immediately. I know, for instance, that I am thirsty now."

René summoned a waiter and ordered mineral water for both of us.

"Thanks, René, but how do *you* know that I'm thirsty? I could be a machine that has no internal feeling, and is merely programmed to say 'I'm thirsty,' even when inside nothing is happening."

"That is in fact a big problem in my dualism of body and soul. (Since Nora can read Latin, she undoubtedly understands what 'dualism' means: a division of the world into two parts.) Ultimately, her conception is dualistic too: she distinguishes between physical things one can see, such as trees and birds, and the feelings that take place in our hearts, as it were. You can see the heart, but not its feelings, and so Nora seems to have gone in a circle. A quite different reality is involved. —Yes, the problem is in fact: how do I know that 'behind' this body there is a consciousness or soul? ('Behind' is a misleading expression, because we may not be dealing with a spatial relationship, since spatial relationships always belong to the physical world. If I go behind you, if I open you up, or even if I make myself little and walk around inside your skull, I can't find your soul.) I'm particularly bothered by this question in relation to animals. When I was alive, I assumed that they were mere machines; now all the animal lovers are after me, and I hardly dare go out in the street, whereas Plato can pick up little girls in the park and no one objects. . . ."

"I think Nora wouldn't like your conception of animals. Moreover, she rightly thinks that ideas must be more than just contents of consciousness."

"Yes, there she's quite right," said a man with a bishop's miter who had slowly approached our table. "In Plato, ideas are a third world beyond bodies and consciousness. Only these frightful modern philosophers have made subjective representations out of them."

"Thanks, Augustine, the next time we'll talk about this further. I have to go now. And René, thanks for the mineral water. It did my body—no, also my *res cogitans*—good."

"I would have bought you an *apeiron* aperitif instead of water," a distinguished man called out to me. "I'm not Thales!"

Now who was that? I am (or at least think I am),

Your Vittorio

Turin, 20 February 1994

Dear Nora,

This letter doesn't follow our plan, since I'm writing it before I've received your answer to my last one. But what I want to tell you seems to me so newsworthy that I can't wait any longer. I arrived here in Turin yesterday afternoon, and after I'd checked into a nice, somewhat old-fashioned hotel, I went for a walk along the banks of the Po. There I met an unusual, middle-aged man with an enormous walrus mustache and an intelligent, meditative face that one might describe like this: a few features, which must have long been fixed, seemed to express great suffering, but over them played a calm, cheerful smile. He was petting a horse that happened to be—I don't know why—on the bank. He nodded to me in a very friendly way, and as I passed him he looked at me with surprise: "Well, well, what are you doing here in Turin?"

"Excuse me," I replied, "do we know each other? My memory gets worse and worse. I can no longer remember where we met the last time, although of course I recognize your face."

"Not formally, young man, we don't really know each other. I've also forgotten your name; I remember only that you are Dinosaur Nora's pen pal."

"Of course, you were recently sitting a few tables away in the Rüttenscheid café. But what are *you* doing here?"

"I'm following memories, and reflecting on some of them! Moreover, I like horses very much."

"And all these churches don't disturb you, Fritz?"

"On the contrary. In the meantime, you see, I've caught on to the old man. I used to think that God was dead, and that I was more or less called upon to provide His philosophical death certificate. I thought I was doing something good for people by making them free. The experience of this remarkable, terrible century, which I've surveyed from above, as it were, has taught me differently—when I think of the criminals who have appealed to me! So I've gradually understood that the old man (that subtle artist) only pretended to be dead, withdrew from this world, in order to set up a terrible but unconditional experiment with it. In His absence He is in a mysterious way present—we know Him more deeply than before!"

"That sounds like a paradox."

"Sure, and it's not easy to understand. You know, only a kid could help you with it."

He winked at me and turned back to his horse, giving it sugar. I was completely bewildered, and after a sleepless night I am asking you: Do *you* know what he meant? Please tell me, it seems very important!

Yours, Vittorio

---

25 February 1994

Dear Vittorio,

Thanks for the two letters! Excuse me for being so slow in answering them, but in the last few weeks I've had quite a lot to do. Anyway, I'll reply to your first letter as best I can.

A question occurred to me: do animals really have no souls? That was also René's question, right? He came to the conclusion that animals have no souls, didn't he? I'm not sure what I should say about that, since many qualities are observable in our dog that really belong to a soul. For example, he can feel happiness, pain, sadness (when he howls), and even a little homesickness. But these are not all the properties of a soul. A soul also has love or understanding. Wait, I just thought of something: animals must have some understanding, because mother animals provide for their offspring, and even scold them. Hmm . . . this is really very difficult. Maybe animals also have a kind of animal soul? Or half a soul? What do you think? Is happiness part of consciousness? Do animals maybe have only a consciousness, and not a real soul? Maybe animals have some kind of knowledge? But you can tell René one thing: animals are certainly not computers!

Yes, Thales would certainly have bought you a glass of water. He considers water to be the original substance of all things. But who was the man with the aperitif? I couldn't read the word that came before "aperitif." Neither could mama.

You know what? After school the other day I went to the train station, as I always do, to wait for the train I take to get home. I sat down grumpily on a bench. I didn't want to wait for the train. But that soon changed: all at once I saw a leg hanging from a branch! That was exciting! Burning with curiosity I ran up to the tree, and saw that the leg belonged to a body. A man! But since when do old men sit in trees and look dreamily toward the north? Astonished, I forgot my manners and said, "Well, now . . ."

No answer.

"Ahem, what . . . what are you doing in the tree?"

"Oh!" he jumped a little. "Excuse me, I didn't notice you."

But when he saw that it was only an eleven-year-old child standing there, he was clearly relieved. "Ah, you know, I like to sit in trees, because up here I'm closer to heaven! Up here it's easier to imagine knowing other worlds than it is down there. Too bad I can't perceive much more than other worlds. I mean, I don't really see them either, but I believe they exist somewhere."

I asked impatiently: "But what do you want to see that you can't see?"

"The Creator! But unfortunately the 'created' can only register the Creator, not perceive the Creator with the senses," he sighed.

Then I noticed what funny clothes he was wearing: a kind of toga like the Romans wore, and lace-up sandals. So when he started talking about the "Creator" and the "created," the nickel dropped: I was probably speaking with Anaximander! But he seemed to have noticed something too. "Might I be speaking with Dino-Nora?"

"You could be right about that!" I said ironically.

He looked at the clock: "Oh, unfortunately my train leaves in five minutes. I have to go now, but perhaps we can converse further at Vittorio Hösle's place. Good-bye, Nora!"

"Good-bye," I replied. And then he went off in a direction completely opposite to the one that led to the train station.

See you soon,
Yours, Nora

P.S. to the first letter:

Now I know what word you wrote before "aperitif": *apeiron!* Papa deciphered it and explained it to me, because he knows Greek. Later I looked it up myself in the encyclopedia. Actually, during our conversation Anaximander could also have used the word *apeiron* when he used "Creator," but he was probably aware that I don't know any Greek. In any case, I find it remarkable that you wrote me something about Anaximander when I met him. Don't you?

Second letter:

You and Fritz have asked me a really hard question! But I'll try to answer it as best I can.

So, maybe God is still hidden in us, because we miss Him. We remember Him, we can still hold on to something of Him, but only a little. However, He wants us to look for Him. That is perhaps the experiment Fritz was talking about. He would like us to notice that we can't do without Him, that when we don't make an effort and don't think about Him and don't obey the commandments, the world comes to an end. Many people hold tight to Him, so far as they can, the faithful, but many other people are destroying the earth. They don't know that God is still there; for them, He is gone. These people have to recognize that it's wrong to be evil and tricky (or whatever). We must help them to see that. That's what God wants to achieve. Only when everyone realizes all his faults and tries to do better from now on will God become more recognizable in us. That means that we still have a long way to go. At this time God is nonetheless in those who constantly wish Him to be here. He is even very near, He helps them. Anyway, I think now you needn't have any more sleepless nights, because that way too we sometimes also notice that God is there. Then we are so "wrapped up" in joy that we have to laugh!

But I'd like Fritz to tell me one thing: Why does a child have to answer this question?

See you soon,
Yours, Nora

P.S. Naturally, I was very happy to get an extra letter from Turin in this way!

Essen, 3 March 1994

Dear Nora,

This René is really malicious! When I got back to Essen I immediately took your double letter, which I liked very much, to the notorious café in Rüttenscheid, found René, and showed him what you'd written. He smiled several times while he was reading it, and here's what he said about your meeting with Anaximander: "Well now, these Greek philosophers have started using—out of respect for little girls that don't know any Greek—a very Christian vocabulary! It's typical that it would be precisely Anaximander who's hanging out in trees.

He was the first member of our group who did not locate the principle we all seek in the immediate material world, but he did not yet elevate it to the sphere of the ideas. Therefore he strives to rise above the earthly, but remains imprisoned in the material. He climbs trees, even though the principle is not to be found in the treetops."

Your reflections on Fritz's question really got him going. "Dear little Nora is truly naive if she doesn't know why children have to answer the essential questions of philosophy. And this already answers her question: in philosophy, naiveté is required more than anything else. Indifference to what other people think, readiness to ask even taboo questions, a certain trust that the right answers are also surprisingly simple—all that is important in philosophy, and in these respects children have fewer inhibitions than do adults. They are less often prejudiced than experienced philosophers. That is because many errors are so great that it can no longer be admitted that they are errors, once they have been believed long enough. Only a philosopher as interesting as Fritz seems prepared to undertake radical revisions. —And there is something else: children have a great wealth of emotions. My conception of God is so abstract that it gives us hardly any joy—not to mention laughter! I should have argued with children more often."

He sipped at his glass of water; after a short pause he continued: "Yes, philosophy needs children. Often, however, children are not yet sufficiently acute. So Nora's observations regarding her dog have not convinced me. How does she know that he feels sadness? He howls. I do not contest that. But to put the matter in my language, his howling belongs to the world of extension. We have here a body that moves, and through the movement of its vocal cords it produces waves that we hear as sounds. But Nora has probably seen mechanical mice that are charged with electricity and then run around. She will find it hard to believe that such things have feelings. So how can she exclude the possibility that her dog is that kind of thing? Moreover: it may well be that mother animals provide for their offspring. But record players also provide us with music—does that mean that a record player has a soul?"

"If I've correctly understood you, you're saying that we really know something like inner feelings only in ourselves. *I am* certain that I am annoyed by your observations just now because *I* am the one who is annoyed. But concerning other beings all I can ever say is: There's someone acting as though he felt joy, pain, etc., but I'm not sure whether he really does or not."

"Yes, more or less."

"Even if I could enter into you to look for your inner life, I still couldn't solve the problem. (Let's assume for a moment that I could make myself that little.) For then I would still see only matter; if I could walk around in your head, I would see nerves that were electrochemically active, but I wouldn't find your soul."

"The first one to put it that way was that gentleman over there in the wig."

"Questions of copyright are not as important as arguments. We'll bring Gottfried into this too."

"Weren't you talking about me?" asked the gentleman in question, who obviously had very sharp ears, for he was sitting fairly far away.

"Yes, we are discussing the mind-body problem, as René formulated it."

"René is correct, of course, when he says that the inside, the soul, the consciousness—whatever you want to call it—is not the same as matter. The form of a body is not the soul, either, as an old gentleman with lace-up sandals taught. A table has a form, but that doesn't mean that it has a soul. However, I am myself absolutely of the opinion that everything that is has an inside, including tables. But it is a very, very vague form of consciousness, such as we have when we are in a deep slumber. In any case, my claim can no more be refuted than can René's claim that only human beings have consciousness."

"But why do you attribute consciousness to *all* human beings?" I asked. "You know only your damned self! I could be a computer without any inside."

René laughed. "I already suspected that last time. You're not a real human being, but only a computer Nora has programmed."

"You insult me, you wound me to the quick!" I cried, outraged.

"This Nora is damned clever; she has programmed you to say that you had pain when anyone catches on to you. But I maintain that from the fact that you think you have pain it does not follow that you have pain. Indeed, my good fellow, I would also tell you this: I am not even sure that you are a real computer. I fear that at the moment I am merely dreaming of a computer. Hence you lack not only consciousness, but also material being; you are only part of *my* consciousness."

That left me speechless.

"You're a computer! You're part of my dream!" I yelled back at him. And just then I woke up and found myself in my own bed! So this time I hadn't really been in the café. I had only dreamed it all! In fact, I had gotten home so late that after I read your letter I immediately went to bed. But two questions were bothering me. First, had I been dreaming earlier, when I thought I was going to the café? And second, am I really only your computer? Please help me!

Yours, Vittorio

———————

Dear Vittorio,

Unfortunately I haven't been able to write (or wasn't able to), because we had to do homework in German, math, and Latin. That is, the Latin homework still has to be done, and I have to practice a lot! Couldn't you please quickly give me your address in America? Then I can write you there to answer your questions, which are extremely difficult. But I can already tell you one thing: you are certainly *not* a computer!!! René probably just wanted to annoy you. Anyway, it was just a dream—don't take it so seriously.

Yours, Dino-Nora

P.S. Can't you come to visit us on Sunday? My parents would also be very glad to see you. It's true there are no tortellini, but the spaghetti is A-1! Then we can continue our conversation about René, etc., "orally." I hope you come. In case you already have something on or would prefer not to come, I'll call you once more.

(By the way, you can also eat the spaghetti with an *idea* of Parmesan cheese!)

I'd be very happy, because then you can tell me whether a computer can think or even doubt: actually, I doubt it.

———————

Dear Vittorio,

Here's the real letter that you've had to wait for so long. I really wanted to write you on Saturday, but unfortunately it wasn't possible because we were sitting in the train to Karlsruhe; my pen would have been jumping all over the page. And on Sunday my cousins had their confirmation. I'm very sorry!

Now, about your questions:

1. Computers and human beings can be clearly distinguished with respect to their origin:

We human beings are created by God.

Computers are "created" by us: they cannot be like human beings, because something imperfect can create only something still more imperfect.

2. Human beings are hungry for knowledge, computers' questions are programmed into them, and for the most part they can only answer.

3. In addition, we notice that something is alive or full of life.

René is right that a computer can also be programmed to laugh. But we can tell whether a laugh is artificial or comes from the soul. We can't rely only on our understanding. We sense many things with the soul.—

I believe that you were not dreaming the last times you went to the café, because, for example, when René bought you a glass of water you were thirsty. That can happen in a dream, but afterward you weren't thirsty any more, the thirst was satisfied, and I think that doesn't happen in a dream. You'd have to get up (sleepwalking) and, while you were dreaming that you were thirsty, get a glass of water, in order not to be thirsty afterward. You would never have gone home "satisfied." But you did, except for the last time, and that time it was in fact a dream.

So I don't really know what to think: first I meet Plato, and then Anaximander, and now . . . Listen:

Last Sunday I woke up very early; everyone else was still asleep. And when at half past eight they still hadn't come, I got up and went out into the cool, fresh, somewhat misty morning air. All the streets were empty. It was very solemn. All at once, as I was standing there, I felt like going to church. I had no idea why, but nevertheless I started out. The birds were chirping. I hadn't noticed it before, but now, since there was something special in the air anyway, their chirping became particularly beautiful. I drew the air deeply into my lungs and every breath filled me with joy. Then I could already see the church. It was big and powerful, but it seemed to invite me to come in. I went inside; it was empty. (I expected it to be.) But I wasn't the only person there for long, because suddenly an elderly black man wearing a bishop's miter hurried in. Gradually, however, he became calm. Then he sat down next to me and said, smiling, "Well, we're probably the only ones seeking God so early in the morning."

"Yes," I replied. "The usual service begins at half past nine."

"The usual," he said.

"Are you . . . are you Augustine?" I asked. I don't know why I asked that, it just came out. Somehow I was not surprised when he answered, "Yes, Nora."

I cleared my throat, and then asked: "But how did you get here? I mean, you've been dead for a long time!"

"Hmm . . . At the moment, time is not important. Sometimes you can see, hear or meet someone, even if a very long period of time separates you from him."

"But doesn't that happen only in dreams?"

"*When* it happens makes no difference. That is not very important. What matters is *that* it happens."

"I see . . . ," I mumbled, somewhat bewildered. But now *he* asked me: "How did you know right away that I was Augustine?"

"Oh, first I knew that something special was going to happen today, and secondly, Vittorio told me what you looked like.

"Ah, Vittorio! There you have another fine example of time: it can go from here to the café, even though a wide expanse lies between them—almost another world. Whenever He wants to, God can make someone traverse great spaces in his life."

"But I wanted to go to church all alone!"

"Yes, but God determined that you should go to church when you wanted to."

"Oh man, oh man, it's already five minutes to ten! I have to go home. Tell me where you live, and then we can have a conversation at your place."

"No, no. Living somewhere is a spatial thing. Just now we are very far away from time and space. Nonetheless, we can see each other again," he said.

And as I looked at the clock, he disappeared. But I did meet Augustine today, too.

René is really too particular about animals. He cannot simply maintain that mother animals are programmed to take care of their offspring! Computers have no empathy, and can't be wicked either! I know that our dog is not a computer!!!

Do you know what book I'm reading right now? "Désirée." Do you know that one? Désirée once almost became Napoleon's wife.

In "Sophie," Mama and I are now reading about Locke. Then come Berkeley and Hume. That's going to be exciting!!!

Mama is going to call you again to invite you to come over on Friday. Then you can see our dog and tell René that he is no computer.

You know what? Sometimes I would like to have a time machine so I could really travel to other times. For example, I could go see Augustine.

See you soon, maybe Friday,
Yours, Nora

Essen, 24 March 1994

Dear Nora,

What a smart, warm-hearted letter you sent me! I just pinched myself to see if I had only dreamed it, and since it really hurt I said to myself that I could have figured out for myself that the letter really came from you, if only because I couldn't have written something so fine myself. Reality is given to us directly, whereas in dreams we have to make it ourselves, and thus we quickly realize that as creators, we are not so good as God. When I was living in India, I learned a little Hindi and could even read a newspaper with the help of a dictionary; I always tried to practice by reading signs. At night I often woke up after the following dream: I was walking through Delhi, and saw in the distance a sign on which I recognized the Dewanagari letters in which Hindi is written. I came closer to read it, but the letters became blurred, and I woke up. My active knowledge of the language was much weaker than my passive knowledge, and when I tried to call up what I had recognized, I failed; the dream fell apart, and reality pulled me back. Thus we have at least *one* criterion for a reality independent of our consciousness: it is better than what we ourselves could have created! And as I said, your letters are like that for me.

I went immediately to the café, because I have a feeling that the dead souls there take almost as much pleasure in your letters as the shades in the underworld did when Odysseus poured out the living blood for them.

"Here he comes, finally!" your (not my) fans shouted. "Where is her letter?" they immediately asked, because I had stuck it in the pocket of my pants. "If you don't have a letter from Nora we won't let you come here anymore!"

I pulled the letter out and handed it around. The philosophers eagerly devoured it (with their eyes). A tall, handsome, sad-looking man was completely delighted with it.

"Good, Nora showed René a thing or two. All these questions about whether someone has an inside or not are ultimately pointless. We have an inner certainty that a dog has a soul and that a computer doesn't, and morbid reflection on why that is so gets us nowhere.

"If I showed the fly how to get out of the bottle, that was because I felt that flies are more than machines."

"However that may be," said Giambattista, whom I had once briefly met before, "one must respect developmental logic. Such radical doubts are not for little children, even if they are as smart as Dino-Nora is. Doubt is not the starting point for either general or particular development, even if it is a necessary transitional stage. Adolescents may sympathize with Descartes, but eleven-year-olds feel more drawn to the ancients and to the Middle Ages, for instance, to Augustine."

"Now, I myself always liked Augustine very much," René said, and summoned me to his table. He immediately ordered water, because he found your argument about satisfying thirst to be a particularly strong one, and he wanted to convince me that this time I was not dreaming. The water really did me good! I seemed truly satisfied, and René said with a smile, "So, your satisfaction really works—like Nora's thirst for knowledge. Both of you really seem not to be computers. It goes without saying that you yourselves know that you are not computers—when I appeared to you in a dream, my problem was how I could know that about you and how you could know it about me. Maybe we have an immediate grasp of other peoples' interiority, a sympathy, that affects the soul directly through its bodily expression. Perhaps I paid too little attention to this capacity in my effort to grasp everything through the understanding. Anyway, may I introduce— this is Augustine, who was, as I said, important for me as well."

I respectfully bowed before a dignified gentleman who was moreover not black at all! I blinked, because you had written about that, but Augustine smiled (soulfully and expressively, that is, not like a computer) and said: "Our friend Nora thought she saw many things that in reality she didn't see at all. For one thing, it was foggy that morning. For another, we all have prejudices and we try to confirm them. For example, Nora knows that I came from Africa, and she thinks that all Africans are black. But I am from North Africa, and there people are not yet black (actually, I'd like to be black, but you can't have everything you'd like). Thus a false expectation led her to an inexact observation. Hence one must in fact always doubt a little, in order to free oneself from prejudices and arrive at certainty.

But can one doubt everything? Now, one thing the doubter cannot doubt is that he himself doubts. Otherwise he could not understand himself. René and I have dealt with this argument a little, though I myself did so rather cursorily in the context of a dialogue, because I at least did not try to doubt that there are other people. But René raised doubt to a principle of philosophy and thus created a whole new human type, and I am not at all sure that it is a good thing for the world."

"And I am not so sure either," René interrupted, "when I see the kind of people who hang out in this café. But I'd like to make one thing clear: I always doubted only in order to move toward certainty; for me, doubting was never an end in itself, but always merely a means to achieve a certainty I did not have when I relied on mere belief. I want to know, not believe!"

"Well, maybe you want too much," Augustine put in, "and even if your argument 'cogito, ergo sum,' 'I think, therefore I am,' is really good—it comes, after all, more or less from me" (oh, this vanity, I had to think, the last vice from which philosophers free themselves!), "it displeases me that you start out primarily from the self and not from God."

"But I do believe in God, I know Him," René replied, "but I am nonetheless surer of myself than of God."

"Really?" Giambattista asked from the next table. "It seems to me that I can doubt God even less than myself. Anyhow, we might die someday (Ha, ha! Of course we can't die, because we're already dead, and our status is quite amusing). It is not absolutely self-contradictory to assume that someday we will no longer exist, but God cannot not exist: He is eternal, we are temporal."

"Ah, yes, time," Augustine sighed. "Is there anything more mysterious than that? Does it exist at all? The past no longer exists, the future doesn't exist yet, and the present is infinitely small. Sometimes I have the impression that time exists only in our consciousness. Therefore Nora doesn't need a time machine; her letters show with what ease she moves through all the ages."

"Well, it might help her, if along with her memories and expectations she also used my 'time machine,' that is, my philosophy of history. Once you have understood how history has to develop, then you can travel across the centuries even more swiftly."

"*Has* to develop?" René replied. "History depends on human beings, and they make their decisions freely."

"Is that so?" Augustine raised his eyebrows and looked ironically around the room. "Nora seems to be of a different opinion. Anyway, in her letter she quotes my statement that God has determined what she wants—and surely I am well founded in assuming that she agrees with me."

"That does not follow from her letter!" René shouted. "Nora certainly believes in individual free will, just as I do."

"How about letting Nora speak for herself?" I asked. "I am going to simply ask her opinion on this thorny question: has God predetermined everything or is there free will?"

"If there is free will, then God is not omnipotent!" Augustine cried.

"If there is no free will, then there is no personal responsibility, and we can only pity criminals," René shouted.

Many others gathered around each of them, until at last almost the whole café seemed divided into two separate camps.

"If I may make a suggestion, dear philosophers! Before you start quarreling with each other, let's hear what Nora has to say."

They all accepted my suggestion. "We'll wait for Nora's next letter."

Yes, that's really what they did, my dear Nora! And I am doing the same.

Yours, Vittorio

Dear Vittorio,

Now my letter of reply will reach you not in America, but in Essen. We had guests for *two weeks* straight. I didn't have a single minute free! How was Easter at your place? Here it was very nice. We found lots of "messengers of life" (eggs). And the church was also very beautiful. Sometimes I wonder why rabbits are supposed to bring the eggs. How did people get the idea of making rabbits the ones who hide the eggs? Funny, isn't it?

Your letter was very interesting, too. I'd never have believed that philosophers would argue so much. To imagine that even otherwise brilliant people sometimes don't give a thought to feelings and understanding, and instead begin a dreadful quarrel about which opinion is the right one ...?!

To Augustine: Dear Augustine, I'm sorry but on this question I side with René. But that doesn't mean that your view is false, because I have only written what I thought, and I am still just a child. Moreover, you have reflected on this problem far, far longer than I have.

I believe that human beings have free will. We ourselves must decide whether our behavior will be good or evil. So that it is not so hard for us, God has given us two things: understanding and feelings. If we make use of both of them we can recognize what is good for us. But only then, I believe. Maybe at the beginning God wanted someone to talk to. Someone with whom He could discuss things. So when He created us, He gave us a free will. He often converses with us in our hearts (souls) and asks us what we have decided. Do you know who that makes me think of ? Socrates: he asks the smartest people so much and so often, and always asks further questions, until the people have to admit that they had acted wrongly, and recognize what was right. I believe that God knows what's going to happen anyway. But when He sees something bad, He goes all out to keep it from happening. He puts himself in our hearts and asks us. Then we have to make our own decision: either a good one or a bad one.

Do you know the story that goes with this? It's in the Bible: the Tower of Babel. In this story God himself admits that He is not all-powerful with respect to our will. When He mixed up people's languages:

"And the Lord said, 'Behold, they are one people, and they have all one language; and this is only the beginning of what they will do; and nothing that they propose to do will now be impossible for them.'"

In my last letter I said that this was probably all predetermined, but I didn't mean it in exactly this way. Because I had really decided all by myself to go to church. Maybe God was right there in my heart, and He persuaded me.

I hope this will put an end to the argument about what I meant, philosophers!

Oh yes, one more thing for Augustine: if there is really no such thing as time, and it exists only in our consciousness, why do we die?

Vittorio, do you know the book "Robinson Crusoe?" I'm reading it at the moment.

All the best, see you soon,
Nora

Essen, 17 April 1994

Dear Nora,

If you only knew the withdrawal symptoms I suffered while I was in the USA! Every morning I went to the mailbox to see if the letter I was longing for had finally arrived—always in vain. Add to that having to put up with being laughed at by my friends, who refused to believe in eleven-year-old girl philosophers. At least yesterday I could find a warm welcome in my café; indeed, the philosophers were dying to hear the latest from Nora. They all listened attentively as I read your letter out loud, and then for a while there was an embarrassed silence. Finally Augustine stood up and said:

"Well, yes, people who believe in freedom of the will are precisely those who are predestined to make this error. In any case we must not take them too severely to task—when they are as young as Nora is, they may still change their minds."

"Quite right, my dear Augustine, we shouldn't argue so bitterly with each other, and renounce feeling and understanding. For we all serve the truth, you in your way, and I—in truth's way."

Augustine seemed on the verge of a furious outburst, but I waved your letter at him, and he suddenly laughed heartily and held out his hand to Descartes.

"But how do you know that there is truth? And that we can recognize it? And that we are capable of sharing it with each other?" asked a very well-groomed elderly gentleman in Greek clothing. "I have very serious doubts about all three of these claims."

"Oh," Descartes replied, "what do you mean by that, my dear Gorgias? Do you assert that there is no truth?"

"I don't assert anything, I'm only considering different things. But let us suppose for a minute that there is truth."

"Suppose I simply asked whether this opinion that there is no truth is itself true. What would you say to that?"

"Socrates, a common craftsman, already plagued us with that question in my own time."

"That may well be, but the fact that it's an old question doesn't mean it's a bad one."

"Let's suppose I replied that the assertion I made—that there is no truth—is true."

"Then, my dear Gorgias, there would be one true sentence, namely the one that asserts that there is no truth, and your view would be refuted."

"Okay, then, I say that my assertion is false."

"But if it's false that there is no truth, then it's true that there is truth. If you immediately take back your assertion, then I don't need to contradict you any more."

"That is why, dear René, I only said that I don't assert anything."

"But if you don't assert anything, how can I take you seriously? How can I argue with you? Someone who asserts nothing is in any case not a philosopher."

"Well, what I'm doing is certainly not nothing. I am simply doubting that there is truth, I don't dispute it, that is, I don't say that the opposite is true. And if I feel like it, I can doubt everything and in that way enjoy my freedom."

"Can you really doubt everything?"

"Well, it could be a dream that you and this café exist."

"Okay, so far as I'm concerned. But can it also be a dream that *you* exist? Consider the following. Your starting point is that you doubt. That means that you are engaged in a mental activity."

"Yes, I concede that."

"But if you are thinking, then you exist—*cogitas, ergo es.*"

Here I broke in: "René, my dear René, in school I learned that you taught *cogito, ergo sum.* Now you are using the second person!"

"Our charming Nora is to blame for that. When she writes that even God wanted a conversation partner, how can I (who am not God, but only want to prove God's existence) shut myself up wholly in myself? Maybe conversation is more fundamental than lonely reflection!"

Frankly, I was taken aback by this—René conceded something here that was very different from his other views, and your casual remark had produced this concession!

At this point Augustine reentered the discussion. "So, René, you won that round. Truth exists, without a doubt. But do we recognize it by means of reason? Or do we have to believe in it?"

"If only it were so easy to believe," René replied. "But we see all kinds of people who believe something *we* don't believe, and we can't all be right. Belief has to be converted into knowledge."

"So you don't believe in the Bible?"

"I may concede that it contains the truth—but what do I do with people like Muslims, who don't consider this book but rather the Koran to be the word of God? And even if we take the Bible as our foundation, it is not at all easy to interpret. Thus we also need reason."

"But isn't reason powerless without belief?" Augustine asked. "I'd like to know Nora's opinion about that, too. Anyway, tell her that her reflections on time impressed me very much. Death is in fact real, even if it goes beyond our finite subjectivity. For that very reason we always experience only other people's deaths. In the encounter with others we become acquainted with our own most important characteristics. But only belief can say what happens to us after death."

"A suitable observation just after Easter," remarked an elderly gentleman in eighteenth-century garb who had an acute and melancholic air and whom I had met a few times before. "I myself am more concerned with peoples' customs than with metaphysical questions, and so I can answer Nora's first question. The Easter bunny and Easter eggs have entirely different origins—the former goes back to pagan conceptions of fertility (think how fast a few rabbits populated Australia), and the latter to the medieval custom of eating eggs after Lent was over. Isn't it remarkable how ideas from pre-Christian times are linked with Christianity's holiest celebration? But isn't it also remarkable that a time like this one, which has moved very far away from Christianity, still celebrates Christmas and Easter? Just as great rivers carry their fresh water far out into the sea, so age-old modes of behavior are maintained for a long time before they die out."

"I hope letter-writing doesn't die out," I said, "and in order to prevent that, I'm going home to write Nora"—which you will have no trouble believing. Warmest greetings.

Yours, Vittorio

Dear Vittorio,

I'm sorry you've suffered such withdrawal symptoms in the USA, but once again my answer is not going to arrive on time. I need more time to think about some of your questions. But soon you will receive my answer.

Yours, Nora

----

29 April 1994

Dear Vittorio,

Many thanks for your letter. Don't hold it against me if I sometimes have to think about your letters for a week or two. I know people get tired of waiting, but I am still just a kid and "mental illuminations" don't come to me so quickly as they do to you clever philosophers. But I hope that in the future I'll be able to "think faster" too!

Oh—thanks so much for the stamps! I was incredibly happy to get them, almost as much as to get your letter. How many friends you must have even in Norway! I have already removed them (the stamps, not the friends) and put them in my album. —

I wish I'd been there to hear the conversation with Gorgias! I would probably side with René again.

René showed Gorgias very clearly that he had to admit that truth exists, no matter how he twisted and turned. Because if there were no truth, we humans would have no goal, and it would really be all just a dream. And I already denied that. For me, truth exists! I believe Plato would have made the same objection René did. He thought life would be impossible without truth, because the eternal ideas are true. You know, you can tell Gorgias is not a philosopher but a sophist.

Otherwise, he would "love wisdom." And reason and belief, too: a good philosopher has both, and Gorgias has only reason. He lacks belief, and thus a goal. Reason builds upon belief. Without belief the world would have nothing you could hold on to. It would be cold and lifeless. People would have no time for imagination: that would be a waste of time and thus unreasonable. That's what the fools who destroyed time in Michael Ende's "Momo" thought, isn't it? And people would probably soon start holding slaves again, because that could be considered reasonable. But that would violate human rights, which can be protected only with belief in true justice.

Consequently: reason is very important, but if it is entirely without belief it can become dangerous.

I hope you are not sad that this letter is so short, even though you had to wait for it so long.

As a consolation I've copied out for you a little piece that I wrote in my essay-book on 10 September 1993:

The World Plantation

Isn't the world a huge plantation,
on which we humans labor,
in order to enjoy the fruits of life, love, and freedom?
The fruit hangs over our heads,
high up on the big trees.
We constantly try to climb up
to get them.
But we always slide down again.
And if we ever get all the way up,
a worm has usually gnawed the roots, and the fruit

that we are closest to falls off
and can't be eaten.
This worm brings in other worms,
shows them how they have to gnaw,
because they don't understand the fruit. —
But someday they will understand
and we will no longer slide down.

Then we are freed from labor. —

—At the moment I'm reading "Robinson Crusoe." Still!

Many greetings, Nora

P.S. Tell the philosophers in the café that I'd like to meet one of them again. It doesn't matter who! He just has to be interesting.

Essen, 3 May 1994

Dear Nora,

You don't have to excuse yourself for spending time on your answers! It's their quality that matters, not how fast they arrive. On the contrary, I admire your composure, since I usually yield to the temptation to write too quickly and to settle matters once and for all. In philosophy, however, things can't be hurried; everything grows at a leisurely pace.

You write that you would like to meet a philosopher. As it happens, I believe you are being observed by one of my friends. (A common failing among us philosophers is that we relate to the world in a purely observational way and seldom participate in it really, actively.) When you wrote your letter, you must have had someone looking over your shoulder—in any case, I was already familiar with it before I read it! "How can that be?" you ask in surprise. Well, over the weekend I was traveling (I not only write too much, I travel too much as well), and when I got into a different train I came into an empty compartment. I didn't really want to sleep, but I must have nodded off a little, because suddenly I looked up and saw two men sitting at the other end of the compartment. They were engaged in a lively discussion. I was bewildered, because I had not seen anyone come in, and the compartment was certainly empty when I got on the train. The two gentlemen did not seem to notice me, and I would have fallen asleep again had I not suddenly heard the way one of them (a big, serious, sad-looking man) addressed his interlocutor (a *very* small elderly man—I think you are bigger than he was—who had a disproportionately large head, and who looked at the world in a clear and cheerful way).

"No, Immanuel, Nora is correct. With reason alone one gets nowhere. This dreadful century—which I checked out of at the right moment, thank God—shows how complete rationality and the worst crimes go hand in hand. How can people so overrate reason?"

"Max, dear Max," the little man replied, "we don't have the same conception of reason. When Nora says that slavery is compatible with reason, I can only strongly contradict her. Practical reason forbids slavery! Practical reason is the foundation of human rights!"

"But why should it be unreasonable to systematically exploit someone's capacity for work, if one wants to achieve a specific economic goal? To be sure, if the slave is lazy and punishment doesn't produce much, free work for hire might be more efficient and useful. But all that depends on the circumstances. I can imagine conditions under which slavery is more rational."

"For you, 'rational' apparently means that something is suitable as a *means* to achieving a given end. But for me reason does not consist solely in evaluating the suitability of means to ends, but rather in judging the ends. When you act in that way, practical reason demands that you pay attention to the humanity in yourself and in others, and that is precisely what is not done in slavery."

"But why should I pay attention to others?"

"Well," and here Immanuel laughed inscrutably, "if you are expecting me to say that you should do so because it is in your own long-term interest, you're wrong. That would be to ignore the sphere of practical reason, that is, of morals. Morality is an end in itself; it serves no other ends. One must not act morally in order to be respected by other people, or even to get into heaven, but rather just because it is moral. 'Act morally' is unconditionally valid; it is a categorical imperative."

Max was silent for quite a long time, and then he said: "So this categorical imperative is something absolute, and it is hard to communicate to our time, which does not recognize anything absolute. But if you are correct, there can be no morality without such an absolute."

"Exactly," Immanuel replied. "Even if this absolute is not in the beyond but in ourselves, it still constitutes the core of our being, so to speak."

"I'm really a sociologist," Max answered, "that is, I'm not so much concerned with what is true as with what people consider to be true.

So it occurs to me that we have different concepts of reason. For you as for your predecessors, reason is something positive, and this does not exclude morality (what Nora calls "belief"), but rather includes it. For me, rationality acts primarily in the realm of well-chosen means. What has happened in European history that could so radically change such a basic concept as reason?"

At that moment the door to the compartment opened, and a man in rustic clothes and the simultaneously deep and wily look of a sly villager interrupted: "The triumph of technology! Since technology has so greatly changed our lives, people think technical rationality is reason. How can original thinking still occur if everything around us is technically enchanted?

"Ah, Martin," Max said, "this enchantment through technological devices is at the same time a disenchantment: the world loses the glittering secret it formerly had. When people still repeated legends and believed in fairy tales, fear and horror may have troubled people, but great passions are better than the indifference that today's mechanical and lifeless world produces."

"But you can't escape them," Martin laughed maliciously, "a destiny drives us on, and you can't jump off a moving train."

"Talk about destiny is itself a fairy tale," Immanuel angrily interrupted, "and Nora is quite right to say that even the worms will someday understand, and then the fruit will no longer get away from us. The imagination of children, who feel in their hearts that there are unconditional moral obligations, can also show us a way out we don't know about."

"Ah," Max groaned, "if only you were right. But this train, which is propelled by modern culture, cannot be stopped. We can travel in it, we can treat ourselves in the dining car, and by looking out the window we can enjoy the landscape—but we can't get off the train, we can't touch the world outside it. Even the windows in this train can't be opened."

For me, that was going too far. "Gentlemen," I said, "that's enough!" And I pulled on the emergency brake. The train stopped very abruptly, and threw me forward; when I had gotten back on my feet, I was all alone in the compartment: my traveling companions had disappeared. But a conductor soon came in, and curtly asked me why I had pulled on the emergency brake.

"I wanted to show the three gentlemen that the train can indeed be brought to a halt . . ."

"What gentlemen?"

"They're gone, leaving no trace behind them."

"Are you trying to pull my leg?"

The conductor was very angry, and there was nothing for me to do except pay a hefty fine. I was beginning to doubt whether I was in my right mind until I read your letter and had the feeling I was remembering—many things I already knew, and thus my experience in the train must not have been merely a dream.

Warmest greetings,
Vittorio

---

19 May 1994

Dear Vittorio,

Many thanks for your letter. I'm so late in writing again; it's good that you don't mind.

Your letter was exciting, though. How did those three men get into your empty compartment? If it had been a dream, you wouldn't have been able to hear them speaking with each other so "reasonably." But you can remember a dream. I once had a dream in which someone suddenly said: "Sometimes you're looking for something, and then it turns out to be not where you were looking for it, but somewhere else altogether!" That's not quite the same thing, but that's what it reminds me of. Kant already said that many questions lead people beyond the bounds of human reason. For example, the question "Is there a God?" That is beyond space and time, and so although we can ask ourselves the question, we can never answer it. Maybe people sometimes look for God where he isn't. —But that's off the subject. I think I've understood Kant's conception of reason a little bit. (Unfortunately too few people act in accordance with morality.)

A question occurred to me: if Kant attributes all moral ways of behaving, such as distinguishing between good and evil, to reason, and considers belief innate or independent, why does he still think the soul is important? Does it take pleasure in the consequences of a moral act? Can you feel pleasure or sadness with the soul? —

Dear Immanuel, if people think morally, don't they believe? Where would the absolute come from, if not from God?

This "absolute" must have come into being before there were people. Maybe this "absolute" is itself part of God. So if we recognize our "absolute," then we really should also believe. Doesn't belief come before reason?

My appeal to the philosophers to come see me again probably succeeded, since I met another one of them again:

We spent the weekend in a little spa in Hesse. There we celebrated the baptism and confirmation of my cousin. We were just a stone's throw from the forest, where there were, of course, many trees, but also lakes, flowers, and shrubs. Unfortunately, there was also a road nearby. It was small, but all the same . . . You could have wonderful walks there, and that was really good for our dog. As we were sitting at the dinner table, I said to Papa: "Papa, I think the dog needs to go out!"

"Okay," Papa said, "go with him, but hurry!"

And so I went into the woods with our dog. I went a little farther, and came to a small lake. Near it was a bench. Everything was so beautiful there that I sat down to enjoy nature. As I was sitting there, I suddenly noticed that someone else was sitting beside me. Strange that I'd not seen him earlier! He was a man with a sorrowful face. I remembered the face, but I couldn't recall to whom it belonged.

Shyly I said: "Hello. My name is Nora. You remind me of someone, but I don't know who it is. Could you tell me your name, please?"

"Of course, Nora. My name is Max Weber."

"Oh, Max! So it's you. Where did you come from?"

"That doesn't matter. What is important is that I am here."

"Sorry. I'm still one of the living, alive people, and so I'm probably too much attached to the law of causality."

"Yes. How do you know me, Nora?"

"Vittorio Hösle described you to me. That's why I could remember you."

"Ah, Hösle, yes. Isn't he the man who recently pulled the emergency brake?"

"Yes, he's the one. He thought he was sitting in the train of technology. That's why he pulled the emergency brake."

"It's a good thing people can put the brakes on that train. I believe you can't do that in the train of technology. If you did, conductors would surely come who would say that there was no reason to pull the emergency brake. They would all have to be previously convinced that it was necessary to pull the emergency brake. And that can't be done. Until the end of the world, there will always be 'worms.'"

"And I believe you are too pessimistic, Max. Why don't you believe in human beings? They were given morality and belief. Naturally, you have to try to put the brakes on! But the problem is that technology is also good. It's not all evil. For example, without ships, trains, and planes, you couldn't travel to other countries. And sometimes you have to do that quickly, or it's very important. Without technology science would not have been able to progress so far. Medicine would be far behind, and diseases like cancer could not be treated. Maybe we have to change the train, I mean its rails. Then it would not lead to the abyss."

"I'm not so sure about that. I don't know if all the computer freaks would go for that. The end of the world will come sooner than we think!"

"But if we believe in Plato's doctrine of the ideas, then the world will not come to an end. The idea of the world is eternal! It will go on throwing shadows. Maybe we will have to begin all over from the beginning."

"Yes, you may be right," Max said, and it seemed to me his face looked more relaxed.

"Oh," I cried, "I have to go quickly, I didn't mean to stay so long. Good-bye, Max!"

"Good-bye!"

And then I quickly ran back to the house. I hope our conversation comforted Max a little. —

You know, Max, there's still time. Technology isn't everywhere. Just think of the beautiful forest. We should just make the nearby road a little smaller. I believe that's enough. — Now Mama is taking the cure, so I mail you my letter. I'm reading a little farther in "Sophie's World" by myself. I already finished with Kant. Now come the Romantics with Rousseau and Kierkegaard.

Yours, Nora

———————

Essen, 24 May 1994

Dear Nora,

As I was attending Whitsunday church service, I was thinking about your letter—for which I thank you—and I had a remarkable experience. In front of me sat a man with downturning wrinkles around his mouth, a big nose, and piercing eyes; he was dressed in clothes that looked to me like those worn at the beginning of the last century.

He seemed very familiar, and I anxiously asked my neighbor who was sitting in the row in front of us. "No one is sitting there," he whispered back, giving me a funny look. "Hmm . . .," I thought, "this is like what happened to me with the three-dimensional pictures, except the other way around. I couldn't see the third dimension, and now my neighbor can't see this spiritual phenomenon that moves in another dimension, so to speak."

After the service I followed him in an inconspicuous way, and sure enough, he headed in the direction of the café you know so well. Shortly before we got there I recognized him—a picture of him is hanging on my bookcase: naturally, it was Hegel. Obviously, on Whitsunday, the feast of the Holy Spirit, even he goes to church. I caught up with him at the door to the café, introduced myself as one of his admirers, and showed him your letter. We went in; the café was almost empty, except for a young man sitting at a table back in a corner. He was small, delicate, almost feminine, with big eyes and a narrow chin.

"A letter from Nora?" he immediately called out.

"Yes, Søren, don't be so impatient," Hegel replied. Then he read your letter through to the end before turning his attention to Søren again.

Surprised, I asked Søren, "How do you know Nora?"

"Well," he laughed, "I'm fond of thinking about myself, and when that gets boring, then I concern myself with other people who think about me. So on Mondays I like to sit in your Kierkegaard seminar (you don't see me, but I'm there all the same, for the inner is not the outer)"—here he glanced at Hegel in an earnest, challenging way. "Since Nora's mother generally defends me against Hegelians, Marxists, and social workers, I often sit next to her, and as she gives you Nora's letters after the seminar and lays them on the lectern, I usually read them before you do. Now, you don't need to get jealous, because at least the last letter you got by mail, since Nora's mother is at the spa—and so I haven't yet read it."

Søren took the letter and withdrew, and thus I was able to ask Hegel, "So, Wilhelm, how are God and the Absolute related?"

"They are, of course, the same thing; I prefer to use the expression 'the Absolute,' but it refers to the same thing that intelligent believers call 'God.' God is the ultimate ground, and if the law of morality is absolute, it is itself divine, a part of God. Or one can also say that God is Himself absolutely moral."

"So God and the moral order go together. But tell me, is something moral because God wills it, or because it is moral?"

"God can will only what is moral, spiritual."

"But then the moral is independent of God's will," Søren called out from his corner. "You thereby destroy God's omnipotence."

"But if something is good, only because God wills it, then God could command something horrible, and it would be good."

"And that's just what He did," Søren shot back. "Think of the story of Abraham and Isaac. Isn't it immoral to sacrifice an innocent child? And yet that's what God commanded Abraham to do!"

"Well, if God commanded me to sacrifice Nora, I would never do it," I shouted. (You can hardly oppose that, Nora, otherwise what should I do?)

"All the same, consider that ultimately Isaac was not killed," Hegel said, "perhaps God only wanted to test Abraham—and perhaps he would have passed the test even better had he said at the outset: 'Dear God, all that is right, but You can't really want an innocent child to be killed, and so I must have misunderstood You.'"

"No," Søren interrupted, "belief goes beyond reason. Practical reason may forbid the sacrifice of children, but belief knows that what is contradictory to reason can be true or God's will."

"Belief cannot contradict reason," Hegel repeated. "Perhaps belief has insights to which reason is blind, but it cannot contradict reason. Otherwise truth would be twofold, a truth of reason and a truth of belief, and that is absurd."

"Credo quia absurdum," Søren chirped.

"What do you do, then, with people who have a different belief?" I asked him.

"Well, they're just wrong."

"How can you be sure that *you're* not wrong?"

"My belief tells me."

"But the belief of others, Muslims, for instance, tells them the same thing."

"Precisely," Hegel said. "We need an authority outside of the various belief systems that allows us to talk with one another, and that authority is reason."

"How true!" suddenly shouted a gentleman in a turban, who looked like he came from the Near East, and who had just come into the café. "The individual religions are imitations of a truth that can in principle be known only through reason. But because human beings are unfortunately not as reasonable as we would like them to be, we can't do without the various religions, even if they often incite hatreds against one another. I am myself an enlightened Muslim—my name is al-Farabi—and I can get along very well with enlightened Christians, Jews, and others. But when someone insists on his own belief and sets himself against truth, it is difficult to talk with him."

"But according to you dreadful rationalists," Søren broke in, "there is only one reason, God's, in which we participate. Then where is the soul, which is always individual and differentiates me from other people? Certain experiences may well be generally valid, but how I feel and interpret them still remains my own affair. Even if there is an objective truth, *I* still have to make it my own."

"We don't mean to deny," al-Farabi and Hegel conceded, "that individual subjectivity is neglected in our work. But in your thought, Søren, objective truth is neglected—and if there were no ideas outside our soul, then we couldn't understand each other at all; each subjectivity would be shut up in itself, without any communication with the world or with others."

"One fixed point we have is that we do understand each other; even if we sometimes misunderstand each other, we *understand* after a while that we have not understood each other and can try another approach. And so I believe," I concluded, "that I absolutely understand Nora and that she understands our conversations, even if it sometimes takes us a long time. But if Nora could delight Max with her balanced judgment of people and technology, then understanding is in principle possible—even when the people involved are of widely different ages and come from very different time periods. There is a world of ideas that is available to all human beings, and through it we can communicate with each other. If there weren't, then of course we could no longer talk with each other . . . and I could no longer write to Nora, which I like to do so much—waiting, naturally, for her reply!

Warmest greetings, Vittorio

Dear Vittorio,
Thanks for your letter. I was delighted with it, yet I am only now answering it. Recently I've had so many rehearsals for the musical our school is putting on, practical examinations, and three more projects in class, that I didn't get around to writing to you earlier. I hope you're not annoyed with me.

I'm enclosing a ticket and also a program for the musical, so you can get some idea of it. I've also learned a little bit about Machiavelli—Mac, I call him. He came up in the play. I'm not sure whether I like him. But I've just heard a little about him. I'm eagerly waiting for your letter; maybe you'll meet him the next time. —

Now for your letter.

I have a question for Hegel: "Dear Mr. Hegel. Can you pray? In your opinion God is not really a person, right? And you can't talk to a 'substance'! You can only judge it objectively. But people don't pray to it. All the same, I want to ask you this question. You might see things differently."

I've already said that if God is moral, then there would be two absolutes—God and morality. That's not possible. Maybe God also has human freedom in His mind. And we can claim this freedom only if we act in accord with God or with morality. If we fought for freedom in another way, for example, with lots of killing, so that our enemies disappeared all around us, then we would still not be free, because we carry a spark of God and the moral within us. This spark would torture us with a bad conscience: then we wouldn't be free either.

God always acts morally! And He commands only what is good, Søren, because Isaac was after all not killed! On the contrary: when Abraham and Isaac were on the mountain God expressly commanded Abraham not to kill Isaac, but to sacrifice the nearby ram in his place. Thus God did not want children (human victims) to be sacrificed. So you can relax, Vittorio, God will certainly not order you to sacrifice me. Also, these days it would be completely absurd to sacrifice either children or animals. —This example was really intended for all human beings. It corresponds to the moral, that is, to reason. Everyone understands that human sacrifices are forbidden. But how any individual interprets history or whether he believes it at all, is his own responsibility.

Reason seems to be more important for people in general than for individual believers. We need reason to communicate with each other and to establish common rules.

Mama is finally back! She was in your seminar again on Monday. I wonder if Kierkegaard sat next to her? Oh, well, at least he couldn't secretly read my letter, because I hadn't yet finished it. Maybe he'll read it tomorrow?

Soon we'll be going away for two weeks. We are going to Italy (= your native land), to the Riviera. That's where we spent our vacation last summer. It's really, really great!

Who knows, maybe I'll meet one of the philosophers there.

Tuesday I get my report card. In Latin I'm getting a B. I know that already.

In "Sophie," Mama and I are reading about Hegel. By myself I really couldn't understand it all.

Yours, Nora

P.S. On the back is my 1st publication:

The Cobra

> There's the snake in its glass case,
> it's being measured with precision:
> One meter fifty from tail to face;
> The cobra's just had luncheon.
> It could easily reach its feed,
> Here snakes can't hunt what they need.
> It doesn't slither free, as it does in nature,
> But just lies there.
> Its fangs emptied of venom,
> A real snake it is no longer:
> Doesn't know how to hunt in freedom,
> Isn't afraid of bullets shot by a hunter,
> Doesn't know how beautiful the forest is;
> Knows only its own cage now,
> That one meter fifty measures.

(I wrote this poem in fifth grade. A few days ago it was published in our school newspaper.)

P.P.S. Are you also going away over the holidays?

On the way to Jena, 22 June 1994

Dear Nora,

Your letter was once again a real pleasure to read, especially since I found it waiting for me last night when I got home from Cologne, where I had just given a lecture on Kierkegaard and Hegel—if I'd already seen your letter, my lecture would have been much better, because everything you said was very enlightening. I also thank you very much for the ticket to Cooltour—it's really too bad my travels didn't allow me to see a performance. I'm sure I'd have enjoyed it very much, not only because Mac appears in it, but also because it seems ultimately to be about personal attitudes toward moral values; seeing you on the stage would have given me great pleasure.

However, I have a question for you: in what way do characters in a play exist? I don't mean the actors, of course, but rather the characters that the actors are trying to represent. The question is relatively easy to answer if you are playing people who once really existed (like Mac), but in many plays characters appear who were not real—like Katherine in "The Taming of the Shrew," which you recently read. *Is* she? Or *is* she not? And what about characters who are made up by a dramatist and play a role in the first act of a play that he never finishes? Since I believe that someday you will be a great writer, but that you will not always finish everything that you begin to think about, I'm worried about all the stillborn spiritual children that you might bring into the world.

When I read your poem about the cobra—which I found very beautiful—I finally understood a remarkable experience I had a couple of weeks ago. As you know, I visited your Mama in the nearby spa. We went for a walk along the river, and there we suddenly saw a rowboat moving upstream. It was being rowed by a man with a big head, meditative eyes, and a red hat like the ones Cardinals wear. He approached the bank, tied his boat to a tree, and got out. He sat down on a stone, took out his pocketknife, and made himself a flute. He began to play it, and then something very strange happened: a cobra began to slither in time with the music, lifted its head, and danced. I didn't notice it at first, because it seemed to be made of glass, transparent, not really material, you had to look very carefully until you saw a reflection, and then you realized it was a cobra. But the uncanniest thing was that the cobra consisted only of its (glass-like) head and tail; there was no middle. Your mother and I were completely bewildered. Finally we asked the man what he was doing.

"Well, first I imitated our Creator," he replied, "and created something that does not occur in nature. Plants and animals have existed from the earliest times, but people make flutes—and thereby we make something new, increase the number of beings. Perhaps you think that being has been fixed forever? No, not at all, we add to being through our achievements in crafts and technology. But flutes have a form and they have matter. It's much more fascinating when poets and artists create something new—because the things they make cannot always be described as material. This cobra is not a natural cobra; it is the cobra in a poem that a little girl wrote last year. But up to now it has existed only mentally, perhaps in one of the girl's notebooks—it has not yet emerged into the public world, and that's why it lacks a middle. But I suspect that will soon change—if this poem is published, our cobra's mode of being will change. It will still be made of glass, but then it will be completely there, whereas now it finds itself in a frightful state, oscillating between being and non-being."

"That's very unusual," your mother answered. "But you are un-usual with your wide-brimmed hat and beard. Where do you come from?"

"I make my home on the Mosel river, and the hat was lent me by the pope a long, long time ago. I search for truth, and try to see God."

"How do you do that?" I asked.

"Well, not with my bodily eyes, of course, but with my spiritual eyes. For me, God is the coincidence of contraries. Look," he said, and drew a top out of his pocket, a top of a kind that is very seldom seen today. He struck it with a little whip and it began to spin faster and faster. "Don't you see first how a given point on the top moves away from us and then comes back? Don't you conclude from this that it is moving and not immobile?"

"Of course, Nicholas," I cried, because I had finally recognized him.

"Then assume that the top will continue to move faster and faster. Point 'A' would then return with increasing speed. What would happen if the movement ultimately became infinitely fast?"

We were silent for a moment, and then we said: "Point 'A' would still be in the same place in relation to the ground."

"But that is also true for what is immobile! Infinite movement and immobility thus coincide. See, in God, all contraries coincide."

"Oh, I'm getting dizzy," I replied, "as if I were myself the top you are spinning. What you say is monstrous. If you were right, wouldn't we have to say that in God good and evil also coincide?"

"Precisely," someone suddenly said as he walked out from behind a tree. I immediately recognized him as Aristotle. "Don't believe this

Mosel fisherman! He destroys logic, the foundation of all argumentation. One proposition is unquestionable: something is either A or it is not A, but never both at once."

"Why?" Nicholas asked.

"Do you question what I say? Yes or no?"

"Yes."

"If you question it, you are saying that I'm not right; but if you are right, then there would be no absolute distinction between being right and being wrong. Thus I would be right."

"I don't dispute that you are right, if disputing it presupposes the law of contradiction!"

"Right—and now I'm really right."

"Oh, Aristotle, I am well aware that one cannot escape the law of contradiction. But it is valid only for the finite world; in God it is transcended."

"Not at all! The law of contradiction is absolutely valid, and thus it is valid for God as well."

"You conceive of God in accord with the model of the created world. But God goes beyond this world, and we need a different power of cognition in order to know Him—reason, not merely the understanding, which is sufficient for the finite world. You're presumptuous to think you can use the same arguments to approach God and the finite world."

Nicholas took off his red hat and waved it excitedly—and then, as your mother probably already told you, the pollen that had accumulated on its brim flew into my eyes and caused a terrible allergic reaction. For a few hours I couldn't see anything, and I couldn't really think either; anyway, up to now I've not been able to figure out who is actually right. But the question is very important to me, and I need your help!

Congratulations on your first, but certainly not your last, publication, my dear poetess.

Yours, Vittorio

---

6 July 1994

Dear Vittorio,

Thanks for your interesting letter. It was really very exciting! I didn't know Nicholas before. Was he a mystic? In any case, I was very impressed by his idea that God could transcend the law of contradiction. —

First, however, I have to tell you how beautiful it is here in Italy . . .
Our cottage is nestled up against a mountain covered with spruce
trees. We have a romantic view of the sea, and it is very quiet. No cars
come here. Only the crickets make noise, but that isn't bothersome.
And how many different beautiful flowers and grasses grow here! But
you must already know all that. You know, to me it all seems a little
melancholic.

Yesterday we were in Pisa. I'd already gone there when I was five,
but I couldn't remember it any more. I'm enclosing a card to you from
all of us. Surely you've been in Pisa and seen its leaning tower, the
lovely cathedral, and the baptistery? Unfortunately, we had only a
little time and weren't able to visit the monumental cemetery. And
Pisa has so many other beautiful churches . . .

All the same, I got at least some feeling of the place, and as I went
into the upper gallery of the baptistery and looked up at the cupola, I
became a little dizzy. What do you suppose people thought about
while they were working on this marvel? I believe they were very
happy . . . The cathedral is also fantastic! And do you know what I noticed in particular? In the beautiful chancel, the muses and the
virtues represented in human form were women. I found that very
odd, since earlier, in the twelfth or fourteenth centuries, the govern-
ment and certainly the whole society had a pretty negative image of
women. Even the muse of philosophy was a woman wearing a crown
and holding the globe of the earth in her hand. In any case, I somehow felt very safe in the cathedral. Right at the end of our visit we
went to the small Jewish cemetery. —(Italy is really a wonderful, very
beautiful country, but up to now there has been a television set in
every café we've been in.)—

Now for your questions.

I believe that characters and plays are like celebrations (for example, Christmas, birthdays, Easter, Ascension . . .). Every time the
play is performed, it is as if the action were just happening. As if it
were the first time it was performed. Holidays like Christmas are also
not celebrated solely to remind us of Jesus's birth. Instead, they are
celebrated to repeat the event that is being celebrated, as if it had just
happened. (I think I didn't put that very clearly.) That was *one* point.
The other one is, I think, that characters are not free. They can't say
what they "want," but are always controlled by the writer. They imi-
tate specific kinds of people.

Okay, so how about the characters in half-finished plays . . . ?

Maybe they are "doubly unfree." I believe they cannot free themselves from their author's consciousness, whereas other characters, by coming into the public world and being known or conceived by many people, can do so. The "completed" characters enter, so to speak, into the realm of eternity, because they are played everywhere, and people everywhere know them. But the "half-completed" ones always remain only in consciousness, and can't get their middles and tails. They have only a head. (Compare: the cobra.)

You also asked if characters really exist. I believe they do, only they live in another world. This world is invisible and makes itself known to us only through the imagination. Maybe this world is just called imagination, anyway? I'm not sure. At least I believe that they (characters) exist. Because they certainly embody an idea as well. Only it is a human idea and not a divine one.—

Now there is still the question whether there are contraries in God or not. I came to my opinion in a remarkable way. On the day we came to Italy, I was strolling around the area, making a sort of "expedition." I went off the path a little and suddenly found myself amid some clumps of dry grass. In front of me there were a couple of large rocks, which had probably broken off the mountain sometime. Now, what did I see? A young man was sitting on the stone and kept looking—with a big magnifying glass—at two beetles that were crawling around on his hand. I found that too funny—I snorted with laughter. Frightened, the man jumped.

"Oh!" he cried.

I was ashamed, and wanted to excuse myself, so I said "Scusi. Mi dispiace." (I naturally assumed the man was an Italian.)

To my amazement he replied: "No problem. I was just so deeply involved in my science."

"In your science?"

"Yes. I was busy finding out what the differences between these two beetles are and which beetle will probably bequeath its characteristics to the future world, and what is most important for its survival. —Who are you?"

"I? I'm Nora. And could it be that you are Mr. Darwin?"

"Yes, indeed, my child. Would you be Dino-Nora?"

At that point I sat down next to Charles on the stone. We talked for a while and ended up discussing your question about contraries. Charles gave me the magnifying glass and told me that I should look at the beetles. I saw that one beetle had longer legs than the other one. But the latter had longer wings and feelers. Slowly I shifted my eyes from the beetles to the ants that were running busily around on the stone. There were brown ones and red ones. It was a real wonder that there were so many different ants. Not one looked exactly like the others. With your question in mind I murmured: "If there are not contraries for God, why did He create the world so that there are always contraries?"

"I wonder that too. God created so many, many contraries—they can't all be the same for Him. In any case, the difference between a human being and animal is certainly not unimportant to Him! But my philosophy doesn't go that far. Besides, I have to go now. In the Galapagos Islands in the Pacific there is still a great deal to be investigated."

"Oh, that's too bad! I would have liked to buy you a cup of coffee."

"Many thanks; perhaps another time. I am convinced that we will see each other again. So until then, good-bye, Dino-Nora."

He put on his green hat and disappeared as if he'd been sucked into the earth.—

So I came to the discovery that there are also contraries in God. I agree with Aristotle. For all of creation consists of contraries. You can see that even in the first act of creation: Out of darkness God created light. Or: He made land appear out of the water, etc.

Moreover, I find what you said about good and evil very enlightening. Because if in God good and evil coincide, then He wouldn't care whether we human beings were good or evil. But He does care. Otherwise He wouldn't have intervened so forcefully in the case of Abraham and Isaac. You can tell Nicholas of Cusa that I have to think some more about his view. Maybe eventually I'll agree with him . . . I find just the thoughts very impressive.

Vittorio, another question about characters in plays occurred to me: can people be described as dramatic characters? Then God would be our author. We would not be free in the sense that God created us as human beings and not, for instance, as angels; that is, we have evil in us. Let's suppose that's so; then could we free ourselves from God's consciousness? Do we find out when our plays or our lives are over? (I believe the question is absurd.)

At the moment I'm reading a biography of Martin Luther King. I finished reading "Sophie" a week ago. It ends in a really exciting way. After Hegel, I read the philosophers Kierkegaard, Marx, Darwin, Freud, and a little about Nietzsche and Sartre.

Yours, Nora

P.S. Reconsider whether you really want to go to America. I think that would be too bad!

P.P.S. Tomorrow we're going to Florence.

---

11 July 1994

Dear Vittorio, here's the card I mentioned in my answer to your letter. As I told you, Pisa made a big impression on us all, even on Bettina. Yesterday we were in Florence, but unfortunately many of the beautiful museums and also the baptistery were closed.

Best, Nora

Essen, 14 July 1994

Dear Nora,

Your letters are among the greatest joys of my life, and your last one, which was about my mother country and was sent to my fatherland, was particularly deep and instructive. All the people you meet! And how you make use of a vacation to look curiously into the beautiful world—and into the world of culture as well as the world of nature. You know that both Plato and Aristotle were of the opinion that philosophy began in wonder, and in fact I believe that today we have so few good philosophers because we have forgotten how to wonder. Only children can release us from this terrible "déjà vu" mentality (naturally, not just any child, but one as alert as you are)—and your capacity for wonder at least (even if you don't wonder at the world) has to amaze every adult.

I was very struck by your observation that in the cathedral in Pisa the virtues and the muses were represented as women. This surprised you because of the negative image of women in the Middle Ages. But if you re-call my first letter, you know that we must not look down on earlier ages too much. To be sure, the Middle Ages recognized no political rights for women. But people were fully persuaded that every human being, man and woman alike, had a defining element, an immortal soul, that would someday have to face its Judge. Virtues ennoble this soul, and of course women can also be virtuous. There is hardly anyone in the modern world who honors and loves a woman as much as Dante did. A multiplicity of relationships replaces the religious pathos of the medieval attitude toward women. I don't claim that this is bad; no doubt today there is more freedom and more equality for men and women; but since justice is the virtue in which moderns have made real progress, we should at least be fair and recognize that medieval people also had their virtues—in the cathedral in Pisa one can in fact feel safer than at the University of Essen.

It's too bad that even in a country as rich in art treasures as Italy, instead of marveling at its wonderful reality, people prefer to watch television. Just imagine that my parents once went with friends to the famous carnival in Viareggio (also in Tuscany). But at the highpoint of this famous celebration they left, saying "We have to go home now—they're showing the Viareggio Carnival on television now . . ." Isn't this a form of madness, in which people give an imitation priority over the reality? But the same kind of madness is involved when we consider this sensuous reality as more real than the ideas that underlie it. People who squat in front of the TV (thank your parents for not having one!) are sitting in a hell within Hell, and are really characters themselves who *on* TV sit *in front of* a TV set. Because, as you correctly write, this whole world is a play whose director is God. I find this idea of yours not at all absurd, but rather very profound. However, I don't believe that we (like Sophie) can move outside God's consciousness. We only imagine we can, and it is God who gives us this impression in advance. What we should hope is that we can move ever deeper into God's consciousness and finally understand what He is really up to in His play. But a full understanding of this is probably denied us in this life.

I'd like to meet Charles Darwin someday. In this hope I immediately took your letter and hurried to the café, but imagine my disappointment when I saw a sign on the door that said: "Even dead (but eternally young) philosophers need vacations. Closed during the summer."

I assume many of them are now in their homelands, hanging around on the squares and so on, where they worked during their lifetimes. This assumption is not mere speculation—it's based on an experience I recently had. I wrote my last letter to you in the train to Jena, and right after I arrived I put it in the mailbox. I was very excited to be in this city that is so important in the history of German

47

philosophy and literature, and I visited, among other places, the cemetery (where for instance the terrible Arthur Schopenhauer's mother is buried), the botanical garden, which Goethe and Hegel often visited, and finally the Romantics' house, where Fichte lived. You can hardly imagine what happened to me there.

I was alone in one of the rooms (the guard had just gone out), and so I approached a big mirror. The person who looked out of it was very similar to me, but he was scratching himself on the head with his left hand, whereas I usually do that with my right hand. He amused me because of this peculiarity, and I took advantage of being alone to offer him my hand. He held out his hand to me in a friendly way, so that we met precisely at the surface of the mirror. But then something really strange happened! The surface began to tremble as if it were made of silver water or quicksilver, and the other hand grabbed me by the sleeve and in no time pulled me into the mirror. I didn't even have time to cry out—already I was in a room that was very similar to the one in which I had been before. But there was one thing about it that was very remarkable: I saw a sign on which was written: ЯОЯЯIM ƎHT HƆUOT OT ИƎᗡᗡIᙠЯOᖷ SI TI. It took me a while to figure out what it said, and the prohibition absolutely made sense! Especially since I suddenly felt that something very odd was happening to me. My first gray hairs turned brown again, my facial muscles tightened, suddenly I no longer had gold fillings in my mouth, my teeth were intact, and I was getting smaller. "What's going on?" I cried out, and then finally I understood: I was getting younger, because in this room—time ran backwards! Can you imagine that? I was afraid the stork would suddenly swoop down and carry me off (in the mirror world, I was told, grownups consider the stork story the only correct one, and only children have other ideas); but fortunately I succeeded in saving myself by quoting an assertion I'd read somewhere in the Romantics' house: "I POSIT THE EGO," I shouted, and stopped shrinking when I was about an eleven-year-old. Relieved, I ran out of the house, but what did I see then? An incredibly rapid transformation was taking place: cars suddenly became horse-carriages, signs fell down, high-rise buildings collapsed and trees grew in their place, people's clothing became completely different. I was afraid to go out of the mirror-Romantics' house, because I feared I might become something strange, lose my identity—which would have been worse than being crushed by a collapsing high-rise, because if I were suddenly to cease to be myself, that would be considerably more awkward than not existing at all. Then I thought of another assertion I'd read in the real house, and I shouted: "I POSIT THE NON-EGO . . ."

Well, life out there became normal again, everything became stable again, but it was a world such as I have known only in my books. Where was I? In Jena, clearly. But who was I? That was my problem.

"Excuse me," I said to a man who was coming toward me, "could you tell me the time?"

The man took a watch out of his vest pocket and answered: "Four o'clock."

"No, I didn't really mean the hour. I wanted to know the date."

"You don't know what day it is? Well, it's June 22."

I nodded to him in thanks, although I also knew that. What I wanted to learn was the year, but I saw that the man would think I was nuts if I asked about that—since normally we know at least what year we are living in! Then I had a clever idea. A man with deep-set eyes and a huge nose was coming toward the Romantics' house; I briefly bowed and asked: "Excuse me, please, how long is it since the French Revolution broke out?"

"It was five years ago," the man replied, "that people demanded that the princes give them back their freedom of thought. For five years people have been fighting for freedom."

"Hmm . . . so it's 1794," I murmured. "Might you be the famous Professor Fichte?"

"The same. So even children know about me?" he smiled.

"I have a friend named Nora who knows not only you, but almost all the philosophers—Dinosaur-Nora, to be precise."

"Dinosaur-Nora? What are dinosaurs?"

"Creatures that existed very long ago, and have belonged to the past for thousands of centuries. Nora herself still belongs to the future. Had I not posited the non-ego, I would have wound up among the dinosaurs myself, but I'd rather go back to Nora."

"Dinos? Nora? The past? The future? Ego? Non-ego? My young friend, methinks you're feverish."

"Not at all. I know you very well and I've read many of your works—your assertions have just helped me get out of a pickle."

"What have you read by me?"

"Well, I've read the 'Groundwork of All Scientific Knowledge,' for example (here he nodded happily), and also 'The Foundations of Natural Rights.'"

Here he stared at me, bewildered.

"You're lying!" he shouted. "You cannot have read 'The Foundations of Natural Rights' yet, because it has not yet been published. I am working on it, but it will be a long time before I've finished."

"I know, I know, your book won't come out for two years. And even then not everything in it will be entirely satisfactory. You could have worked considerably longer on your proof of intersubjectivity."

"You little monster!" Fichte burst out. "You can't know thoughts I will develop two years hence!"

"I can do a lot more than that. I can predict that you will change your views in fairly important ways—for instance, regarding the French Revolution, and also regarding the ego."

"But then my freedom would be an illusion! If what I am going to do in the future can already be foreseen, then in reality I have no freedom."

"Well, I come from the future, actually—and that's why for me you are in the past. And no one can change the past— not even God, presumably; I'll have to ask Nora."

"The past is in fact unchangeable, but not the future."

"That's strange," I replied. "It's implausible that absolute immutability is a property of the past, but not of the future, especially since the distinction between past and future is relative—relative to the present in question. What is now the future will someday be the past."

Fichte reflected for a long time, and then he said: "If there is freedom, then it is also dependent on this present. And freedom is endangered if by traveling through time you can shift at will the distinction between past and future. For the sake of freedom: time must not run backwards! This kind of travel is categorically forbidden! Get out of here, or I'll resort to force."

"He's prepared to do anything for the sake of freedom," I thought to myself, and began to run—right back to the mirror-Romantics' house, because it barred my way out of there.

"I'm going to confiscate your contraband out of the future," Fichte yelled after me. Completely terrified, I ran into the house until I stood before the mirror. No exit any more, I thought with dismay—

then my mirror-image's hand grabbed me and pulled me through the mirror . . . I was back in Jena, 1994, barely thirty-four years old.

The guard scolded me: "You're not supposed to touch the mirror. It's historic!"

"I know, I know," I said, "never again! You're absolutely right!"

The moral of this letter is this: be careful with mirrors.

All the best, Vittorio

P.S. I'd very much like you to tell me if I'm the same person who was in the mirror world. I had an entirely different body. What constitutes our identity?

---

27 July 1994

Dear Vittorio,

I would have found it extremely exciting if you had remained an eleven-year-old boy, because then we could have gone to school together. But I already told you that, when you were at our house over the weekend. I really enjoyed your visit. And now I'm also reading "Through the Looking-Glass." I like it very much, but I still don't quite understand it. I'm going to have to ponder it a bit longer. I just find it odd that the characters always look down on Alice so much even though they are themselves much dumber than Alice. But maybe that has something to do with her country or with "backwards customs"?

Your story about the carnival frightened me—to think that people would put its imitation first. Many people are actually not grown up. For them, it's enough to see what other people are doing, they never think of doing anything themselves. They probably don't even want to! But maybe it's only modern technology that makes people so unimaginative. We'd really get along just as well without it. But many people have become so used to the sleepy, comfortable way that they can't find the meaning of life without technology. Thus every age has its good and bad sides. The Middle Ages was lacking in justice, and our modernity in imagination, ideas, and community. So because many tasks, such as those connected with harvesting, are no longer carried out by many people working together with rakes and hayforks, but rather by an individual working alone with the help of a tractor, loneliness results. We have to be careful that modern technology doesn't become more important than we are. And that we are not subordinated to it, rather than the other way around. Do you know what film that makes me think of? Charlie Chaplin's "Modern Times." We watched that once with our German teacher, and I liked it very much. You have seen it, haven't you?

What you said, that we should try to move deeper into God's consciousness and not to free ourselves from it, struck me as very plausible. If we could move outside God's consciousness, I think we wouldn't be real, contented human beings any more. Maybe then God's breath of life would be extinguished in us. We would be without spirit or soul, like animals, if we existed at all.

And so I also find it much more exciting to immerse myself in God's consciousness, in order to experience the meaning of our life completely. But you said that we probably can no longer do that in our present life. That made me a little sad, but then I reflected that we might learn it after our deaths. I believe that we come back to God after our deaths. Just as we came out of God's mind, so we return to Him. In any case, I want to help human beings to learn the truth as soon as possible.

Now for your questions:

1. I don't believe that God can change the past. He can at most mitigate it, by forgiving an act, or He can punish past acts. For example, in Paradise: He punished Adam and Eve for their forbidden act of eating the fruit of knowledge by driving them out of His Paradise. And from that time on human beings were free, and He could no longer control them. But He had created humans in time and space, and if we speak of the past, we cannot speak of it in relation to God. He always lives in the present, and for Him the past is perhaps also present . . . But wait! I'm getting dizzy. I don't know whether what I just wrote is right or not.

2. Yes, I definitely believe that you are the same person who met Fichte in the mirror world. You had the body of an eleven-year-old, but since you shouted "I POSIT THE NON-EGO," you must not have lost your identity as a thirty-four-year-old. (When you were eleven you certainly hadn't read "The Foundations of Natural Rights," had you?) Identity constitutes the current present. The question is only whether you are the same person. And therefore what Fichte said is probably also right: that one must not shift one's "present" from one time to another, because otherwise freedom is endangered. And since God has freedom in mind, we must absolutely hang on to it. You don't want to touch another historic mirror, either, "for the sake of freedom!"—

So, now I have to jump into bed as quickly as I can!
Tomorrow I'm going to a riding school for a week.

All the best, Nora

P.S. Do you know what struck me about Anne Frank? That she has so much, so amazingly much in common with me. At least in her thoughts.

P.P.S. If time runs backwards in the mirror world, is there no freedom there?

Essen, 2 August 1994

Dear Nora,

As always, I was delighted by your letter, which I received today, and I want to answer it right away (even if I'm naturally grateful that you were a little late in replying—otherwise the post office would be overburdened and break down altogether!). Yes, it also seems to me that it wouldn't be at all bad if I had remained a boy—mainly because then I could have grown up with you. But wait! If I were exiled in the mirror world, and transferred into the eighteenth century, I wouldn't be able to go to school with you—and so I'd rather live in the late twentieth century and already be thirty-four years old! I wouldn't want to give up the pleasure of seeing you. Moreover, the difference in age that separates us has the great advantage that I can help you understand many things about the world that still bewildered me when I was eleven years old (I hadn't yet read Fichte, even though I wouldn't absolutely say that reading him really bewildered me; in addition, my meeting with him in Jena left me with an unpleasant taste in my mouth—the man has a tendency to be violent). That is one of many reasons why you should be thankful that you grew up with a grandmother in your house—in that way you acquired a deeper view of the past and a lot of help in understanding the world.

You are quite right in saying that in the modern, technological world there is a dreadful tendency toward loneliness, but it is still resisted by many spiritual and moral people united by a bond of friendship that also includes people who have long been dead—like Anne Frank, for instance, in whom you recognize something of yourself. (What, exactly?) To say one more thing about childhood, I sometimes have the feeling that I am also in many respects like an eleven-year-old—I don't want to give up a certain naiveté and spontaneity, and you help me keep them from running out. It may be that many odd characters look down on us as they do on Alice, for unfortunately it is not only in the mirror world that stupidity and arrogance grow on the same tree; but since we know that, we won't let it bother us any more.

I think what you say about God's knowledge is very true, even if it makes you dizzy. I believe in fact that for God there is only an eternal present. He is outside time, and He already knew a billion years ago that Nora K. is at a riding school in Westphalia and constantly senses, when she is riding, that Descartes is wrong to deny that the higher animals have consciousness. But here we encounter a problem. If God knew so long beforehand that you would go riding, can you still really have freely chosen to go riding? Or are all your choices not predetermined by God? You remember what excitement about this question there once was in the café. A well-known argument for the view that everything is predetermined by God is precisely the fact that the past cannot be changed (even by God); but it is odd that the future can be changed, particularly since the boundary between the past and the future is constantly shifting: what was yesterday the future—today—is the following day the past. If there is no ontological difference between past and future, then it is hard to understand freedom.

A few hours ago, I was banging this question around in my mind (or rather: this question was banging around inside me) as I walked, holding your letter in my hand, toward the café in Rüttenscheid. I had forgotten that it is closed during the summer, and only when I had my hand on the door handle did it occur to me that I would probably not find anyone there. But strangely enough, the door opened, and I walked in. The café seemed to be completely empty, but a moment later I noticed that two large mirrors stood facing each other at the end of the room. Despite your warning I felt myself drawn to the mirrors as if by magic, and I hurried over to them. A strange figure emerged from a dark corner next to one of the mirrors. It was a little man who looked around him in a strained way, and whose thin, knife-sharp lips were smiling ironically. Nonetheless, there was something menacing about him, and I immediately froze when he quietly, but in a commanding tone cried: "Stop! Give me Nora's letter!"

To tell the truth, I found this insolent, and I did something maybe I shouldn't have done (what do you think?)—I lied.

"I don't have a letter of Nora's on me," I replied, but he came up to me impatiently, pulled the letter out of my pocket, where he had spied it peeping out, and said to me sarcastically: "Now you really no longer have it on you." He read it through quickly—amazingly quickly; toward the end he shook his head and said "Poor kid! Her answer to the identity problem is very weak. It's circular—Nora is going in circles. Identity means self-sameness—and to that extent she explains nothing when she says that for identity it is important that one be the same. That's trivial. I'd like to know this: why am I the same? Does the *body* have to be the same? Or can I be the same even in a different body? Do I have to be able to *remember* my earlier experiences in order to be able to say that I am the same as I was in San Casciano? But let's suppose that I had forgotten everything about earlier times— would I still be the same person?"

"Yes, Mac," I cried—for in the meantime I had recognized him— "you would really be the same, even if your body were different, even if your faculty of memory were to fail you. But your behavior in relation to the world has not changed. Your will to power remains exactly the same. Why are you hanging around here, anyway? I thought even dead philosophers went on vacation. And what are you so curious about in Nora's letter?"

"So far as your first question is concerned, I can only tell you that a man who is concerned with power cannot, unfortunately, afford to go on vacation. I have to scheme constantly and everywhere, in order to foil plots; I have to put together conspiracies, in order to uncover other conspiracies. Even at night I can hardly sleep. Vacations, vacations! They're for those contemplative lazy-bones! I am responsible— I can't allow myself any free time. If you knew how many German philosophy professors are constantly appealing to me for advice! The time is past when people could still refer to God; these days, it's a matter of power."

"And what about my second question?"

Here Mac became somewhat embarrassed; he even blushed.

"Well, you know, in another letter (reported to me by one of my countless agents) she said she didn't know yet whether she liked me. I'm curious to know whether she has reached a conclusion."

"Why?"

"Frankly, because I'm not sure myself."

"Whether she should like you?"

"No, whether I should like myself. I'm not entirely at one with myself. That's also why I'm so interested in the question of identity. Sometimes I almost hate myself—even though the hater and the person hated are one and the same. How is that possible?"

Mac had moved backward again and was standing between the mirrors, so that he was reflected repeatedly (an infinite number of times?). Then something totally uncanny happened. The mirror image on the right side suddenly began to talk.

"I'm really a monster," it said, "I've given tyrants brilliant advice about how to oppress innocent people. Violence, lies, treachery—I know all the tricks. And I can tell you this: if you don't use these tricks, you'll soon find yourselves butchered by those who do. People are evil, and therefore you have to be evil to them."

Then the mirror-Mac gave a cruel laugh. But on the other side another mirror image began to speak.

"People think I'm brutal. But in truth I have only described the brutality of evil people. People think I'm in favor of tyranny. But while I listed the cruelties of tyrants in my little book, in doing so I performed a service to common people. Tyrants don't need my help—they do what I described, and go on doing it. It would be in their interest for me to keep quiet. If I were really Machiavellian, I'd have written only edifying religious works and distracted people's attention from the tyrants' tricks."

"Thanks, Mac," the first mirror image cried. "Now everyone thinks I'm a good fellow, if not a courageous one. That's very convenient for me. That way I can worm my way into the confidence of the oppressed, the better to deliver them into the hands of the tyrants."

"Oh, Mac," the other mirror image replied, "you really are a marvelous actor. I almost betrayed you to the tyrants, and now you've saved the situation again. Congratulations!"

"If you don't immediately stop attributing moral intentions to me, and finally understand that for me it's a question of power and nothing else, I'll have you killed!" Mac #1 yelled, his face contorted with rage.

"Oh, Mac, your goodness is infinite! You're ashamed to present yourself as an upstanding person, and so you play the savage," Mac #2 answered, doubled up with laughter. "I'm suspicious of anyone who talks too much about morality, but you're my idol!"

"Here the real Machiavelli, who had stood motionless between the two mirrors, threw me a despairing glance. He walked forward, and the mirror images vanished.

"See why I've got identity problems? I really don't know who I am any more! Am I a benefactor or a monster? Should I hate myself or love myself? Only Nora can help me here."

At this point Mac lost his composure and threw himself sobbing onto my breast. "Talk with Nora about me. I must know whether she likes me or not!"

"Calm down, Mac," I said, "it's not so bad as all that. The world is better than you think, and Nora can solve your problem as well. I'll write to her today, and you can have her answer—and there's no need to send your agents to steal her letter this time: I'll be glad to show it to you."

I went home and wrote you right away, because I didn't want the poor guy to have to wait too long. He's really suffering.

All the best,
Vittorio

---

23 August 1994

Dear Vittorio,

Many, many thanks for your letter and for the beautiful stamps! Now I'm in seventh grade. And my new subject is English. I'm having a lot of fun with it, and that's good, because later on I'll have to be fluent in English in order to get around in the world. I also find geography fascinating! Latin is also good, too, but now we're dealing with the accusative cum infinitive, with infinitives, and with future participles. At first I didn't quite get it, but now I understand it.

Now for your questions.

1. How is Anne Frank like me? . . . I think sometimes she's really angry and doesn't know exactly why. I often feel that way too. In addition, she sets life-goals for herself: she'd like to be a journalist. That's something like being a writer, which I think she would have ended up becoming anyway. She likes to learn things, and tries in every way she can to find out something about the world, even if she has to live hidden away in the attic. And she has so many thoughts like mine, for example, that so long as you have nature, life is wonderful . . . Anne Frank also philosophized, which I love to do.

She always says that in order to get along, she has to build her own inner world, and I think that too.

She also likes to write stories. So all in all, if we had met we would surely have become friends.

2. You know, you wrote that God might have known in advance that I was at a riding school. (It was great, by the way.) But I don't like that much. It would correspond to my earlier letter, but all the same I'm not sure . . . Instead, I now think that God's "life" and our "life" must be very sharply distinguished. The two "worlds" are very different and mustn't be confused with each other. God lives in his world in an eternal present. But when He wants to communicate with human beings, He has to descend into our world. He does that and can have pity on us. If God knew everything in advance, our freedom of action would be threatened. Then it wouldn't be my free choice to go to a riding school or not. Not completely, anyway.

3. It's really strange that the future is changeable but the past isn't. However, I think there is an ontological distinction between past and future. You already know that I don't believe in God's foreknowledge, and that goes along with my opinion here. The future is something human, not divine, and therefore it can be the opposite of the past. The important thing is precisely that the past and the future are constantly shifting!

4. Okay, okay, dear Mac! I probably made a mistake, but you don't have to get so terribly upset over it. I mean, everybody makes mistakes. It's good there's a future—that makes it possible for us to improve. Moreover, you made your share of mistakes in your life!

And I have to say: you have a pretty horrible and shifty side! But all the same, you can rest easy: I feel a certain sympathy for you! You know why? Because (1) you can understand that you've done wrong, and (2) you are passionate. You see—you can't avoid the good, because you still have good sides to you. So far as evil goes, your bad mirror image is almost defeated. But you did teach the powerful new tricks. I think you can hardly talk your way out of that, but—as I said—we have a future!

Now I've got another question for you, Mac: what's more important, power or good influence with people?

Well, now, what philosophers are always appealing to you? I can tell you this: Vittorio isn't one of them!

And so far as your self-esteem goes: just think about whether you've ever done something really good! If you haven't, do everything you can to achieve peace of mind, and if you have, you've got something you can hang onto, something to cherish. And you also have friends now!—

(Vittorio, when you go to the café, tell him that this part of the letter is addressed to him!)

Yesterday I finished "Ben Hur," and now I'm reading a kind of biography of Anne Frank by Ernst Schnabel. In addition, I read "your" article in the newspaper. I found it very good, but it made you seem a fabulous star, and I don't think you're really like that.

Also, doesn't it say that you would have liked to live in earlier times? (I've sometimes wanted to do that too.) But that isn't like you either, because you always base yourself on the facts. You only want to take up old thoughts (for example, about Hegel) again, right?

Hu Nam called us recently, and we may soon go to Hamburg.

Too bad that you have to go to Spain. Nonetheless it will certainly be very beautiful there! Mama already told me what your route through Spain and Portugal will probably be. Will you write to me from Spain? Unfortunately I don't have your address. You can send it to me, can't you?

See you in a month at the most,
Nora

Aranjuez, 31 August 1994

Dear Nora,

Your letter came at just the right time, because my vacation started a few hours later. Clearly, I was rather moved when I read your declaration of sympathy with Mac, because I immediately understood how important it would be for him to read your remarks, and that I could hardly keep him waiting until I came back from Spain. On the other hand I still had to pack up, and it seemed I wouldn't have time to take your letter to the café. I was looking glumly at the table when I suddenly heard a noise behind me and Mac called out: "Don't worry about the time problem. If the mountain won't come to Mohammed, Mohammed will have to go to the mountain."

I was dumbfounded. "How did you get into my apartment? How did you know that Nora's letter would arrive today? Are you a mind-reader?"

"I can do that and much more besides. But would you please hand me the letter? I'm very eager to read it." He skimmed the first part and then read very carefully the part that concerned him.

"Hmm, hmm, then this nice girl may like me after all. Good, good. I like her too. But I have just realized that peace cannot be achieved by good words alone. Why don't people in the state kill each other? Because they are afraid of being punished. But they feel this fear only so long as they are punished when they commit crimes. Hence the prince (or whoever represents the state) has to be really fearsome. If a cat's good-naturedness makes him weak, the mice will play, and there will be conflict and soon bloodshed. If we want to protect all life, we have to be in favor of a strong state. All the tricks I recommend are directed to this goal—I am a moral person, even if the moralizing of people who only talk but solve no problems gets on my nerves."

At that point I suddenly heard a noise in the next room—a book seemed to have fallen from the shelf. I looked into the room; the book was Thomas Hobbes's "Leviathan." From the pages of the open book a little man walked out, and grew larger, but not to a size greater than that of a child. He winked at us ironically and said: "A very stimulating discussion—may I jump in? Excuse me, my friends call me Tom."

"My dear Mr. Hobbes, I had no idea that people who subscribed to your philosophy could have friends. But you are welcome to participate in our discussion."

He gave a chuckle that sounded like a whinny, and then threw back his head and cried: "I would beg your little friend, whom I've run across once or twice, but who has studiously ignored me (so it's her own fault if she complains that she doesn't meet philosophers any more), that is, Nora of the big dinosaurs, to please understand two things. First, she herself has written that she's angry about something. What do you do with anger? You get into quarrels with other people, and end up resorting to violence. In actuality, human beings are very aggressive animals, and their lust for conflict is limited in only two ways, the first of which is law, which precisely determines what belongs to whom. It makes no difference whether its regulations are just or not—or rather, they are just by definition. For however these regulations are framed, they put an end to conflict. Of course, they can do so only if law is backed up by the greatest power, and now we're talking about the state. Mac and Tom Inc. represent the interest of the state—on moral grounds, of course." Here again he whinnied like a horse. "Secondly, I don't think much of Nora's distinction between power and influence. Influence is also a form of power—everyone wants power, wants to have an effect. It's just that some people impose their will by means of weapons, while others do it through words—like us intellectuals. My impression is that our little Nora will also become an intellectual." Here he shook with laughter until tears came to his eyes.

"Now listen here, Tom," Mac replied, "Nora has nothing against power. For her, the issue is *to what end* power is employed—and that is the moral problem. Presumably she reproaches us for simply legitimating state power."

"Whatever. I've still got to pack. Take off, or I'll show you who the legal owner of this place is." That produced an effect, and both of them immediately disappeared.

The power of language seems to me in fact to be a very important problem. Today, journalists have quite a lot of power—most politicians do only what they think public opinion wants. Therefore journalists have a special responsibility to report precisely and accurately. The journalist who wrote the article about me in "Die Zeit" was conscientious—he just didn't know me as well as you do. On the other hand, in the enclosed article, the one girl with many letters I mentioned (three guesses who that was) was turned into many young readers of "Sophie's World." As if what counted was the number and not the quality of the letters!

My trip to Spain began with a big disappointment. The day after I arrived I was going up an escalator when I was approached by two Algerians, one of whom had only one leg, and seemed to be having problems getting off. I held out my arms to help him, and when I did he took the opportunity to steal my wallet, in which I had Spanish currency worth about 600 Deutschmarks (I'd just changed money), my passport, etc. A passerby told me to watch out, but it was already too late. Accompanied by a Brazilian I had met, I chased the two-legged robber, and caught him before he got away. He fought like a cat, my glasses flew off, and we rolled around on the ground until we ended up holding each other. In the meantime, the other robber limped away, and two of his accomplices took him away in their car. When the police finally got there, it turned out that the other man had the money—I'll never see it again.

I was very annoyed with myself; during all my travels in India, Latin America, Russia, and Tunisia that kind of thing had never happened to me—partly because I had hidden my cash more carefully. But in Spain, where I had lived for a year in 1972–73, I thought I didn't need to be careful. However, the country has changed a great deal over the last twenty years, and unfortunately not always for the better. In the evening, as I was sitting dejected in my hotel room mulling over what the police had told me—that most of the robberies of this kind were committed by North Africans who were living here illegally, I suddenly noticed that an elderly, bearded man was sitting on the windowsill. I jumped, but he gave a friendly laugh and said: "Don't be afraid, I'm a friend. You ought to recognize me, really."

"I can't remember you," I replied with embarrassment.

"Why are you in Spain?"

"Well, I was invited to a conference on Ramon Llull, that strange, brilliant fellow from the thirteenth and fourteenth centuries on whom I've done a certain amount of work."

The old man laughed heartily. "A conference on Ramon Llull almost seven hundred years after his birth! Who'd have ever imagined that? During my lifetime people thought I was crazy, and now professors come from all over the world to discuss my work! Well, this world may be really nuts, but I like it all the same. It's God's creation, after all, and it's sinful to get too upset over everything that's wrong with it. You're annoyed about having your stuff stolen? Are you angry at North Africans in general? That's understandable, but not very smart. Sure, you were right to fight with the guy, because you can't let injustice go unpunished. On the other hand, in your life you've had so much good luck that you have to just calmly accept this loss. Have a little more dignity, even if you don't have any sympathy with the one-legged man.

"Ah, these North Africans . . ."

"I know North Africa better than you do, my friend, and even if the current situation is alarming, I can tell you that Islam is a respectable religion, and that I learned a lot from Arabic philosophy. You know that I wanted to convert Muslims to Christianity, and I used to enjoyed debating with them. We agreed that there was only one God, but we Christians also believed in the Trinity and in the Incarnation. At the time, I tried convince them by rational arguments, because I soon understood that appeals to belief were of no help, since Muslims have a different belief. It's too bad that there's so little dialogue between Christians and Muslims these days. Since the beginning of the modern age our culture has become much more powerful than theirs (which does not mean that we're right, obviously), and that makes discussion more difficult. Presumably, belief in the Incarnation resulted in a different understanding of history—it would be possible to see that as progress. Ask your friend Nora what she thinks about the Trinity."

"You know Nora, too?"

"Of course. I like children. It's true that after my vision I left my family as well, but for my son I wrote a book of his own.

"Tell me, Ramon, how should we deal with Muslims?"

"Talk, talk, talk. Mac & Tom are right: Peace requires a monopoly on power. But that's not enough. People also have to come to an agreement about basic truths. Let's remind Arabs of the power of reason in their own tradition. Then they may see that our discussion is an imitation of the triune God. So—that's it, Vittorio. Have a good Llull conference! I have to go continue a discussion with a Buddhist."

My bitterness disappeared after this encounter, and amid the wonders of Castille I constantly think how much Spain owes to the synthesis of Western and Islamic culture.

Yours, Vittorio

---

25 September 1994

Dear Vittorio,

That was an exciting letter! It isn't every day that philosophers crawl out of books and suddenly stand in the room or just sit on hotel windowsills. And then your experience in Spain . . . It was surely disappointing for you to reach out to help someone and get an empty pocket in return! It's terrible how people's readiness to help others is exploited for crooked purposes. However, I think it's good that you chased that creep and beat him up, but it's too bad he didn't have the money. You know, if all or most people acted in such an underhanded way, soon we wouldn't be able to help anyone with a clear conscience, if we helped anyone at all. But fortunately you had another identity card and were able to cross the border. —

Do you know what? I don't care for Hobbes at all. I've got no time for him, I think. He's too ironic and—oh, I don't know how to put it—too spiteful. Mac appeals to me much more. In addition, anger doesn't have to end up in quarrels. And even if it does—quarrels are important.

We just have to know *how* to quarrel. Force has no part in "real" quarrels. Quarrels might even be called exceptionally lively and entertaining discussions. Ultimately, however, people have to get along, even if they don't find a mutually acceptable solution. By expressing our opinions, giving arguments for them, and listening to our opponent's arguments for his position, we feel free again, or at least different from the way we felt before the quarrel! If force is brought into the quarrel, then we have very stupid opponents who are out of arguments and leave the subject completely behind when they resort to force. Unfortunately, however, this happens, and here we need a state that can punish the use of force. I believe that, too. But the law itself has to be just; otherwise it provides no sort of model, but only makes people afraid that if they commit violent acts they will be paid back with violence. That's not the point. Or do you find the torture practiced in Turkey just, Hobbes? I don't at all!!! Hobbes, you subscribe too much to the motto, "the means justifies the end," and that is something I don't like. No doubt materialists (like you) disagree. Oh, yes, there are two different kinds of power: (1) power that results from the fact that you have a certain dignity and a certain influence on people (for example, Martin Luther King), and (2) power that you have because people are afraid of you and do everything they can to avoid getting into your bad books (for example, a king).

I've puzzled over your question about the Trinity, but I can't believe in it as the Christian Church tells us to. I find it a very lovely idea, but isn't there even something pagan about it? A man, that is, Jesus, as God? I do believe that God can appear in three functions, namely as God in the other world, where oppositions are transcended and where time also plays no part; and as the God who descends among his creatures, among humans, goes through time with them, and rejoices and suffers with them. And also as the God (still the same) who has a spark in humans, who breathed his spirit into humans and who offers them salvation. I really agree with all this, but is Jesus also God? I still don't believe that. Jesus himself prayed to God. I believe God chose him as a model for human beings, but I don't believe he was God's son. He was "just" linked with God in a special way. And he knew that. To that extent I don't entirely agree with the Christian Church, Llull! (I think it's good that you calmed Vittorio's anger.) But perhaps you can explain to me, Llull, what the Trinity is all about, or better yet, how you see it. You know, Llull, I also think we should talk a lot with other people (especially with Muslims). We have to talk together, discuss things, and find solutions. It will soon no longer make any difference whether one is white or black, Jew or Christian, Chinese or Indian, and so on. But it will be a long time before humanity understands and observes that. I'd really like to help bring peace to the world. Maybe I'll be able to do that. But that's in the future. —

It was very nice being at your place yesterday! The tortellini were delicious (as always!). It's important to know how to cook as well as how to philosophize. It's too bad that you're going away again. During spring vacation I'm probably going to Hotti & Co. I'm already looking forward to it.

You already know that at the moment I'm reading your "Ugarit." So I'm going to run to the mailbox and mail my letter to you!

Yours, Nora

On your twelfth birthday

Dear Nora,

First of all, my best wishes on your twelfth birthday! That is a very fine number that you've now reached—it indicates a certain rounding-out and completion. Gradually you're leaving childhood behind and moving into adolescence: you'll encounter many problems, but I'm sure you'll overcome them and do great things with yourself and for the world. Everything you wrote in your school newspaper pleased me, and especially the article about the rain forest. You clearly analyze the problem, you're prepared to draw the consequences for the way you conduct your own life, and you have the optimism and energy to move others to do the right thing. If there were more Noras, the world would be better off! Anyway, for the coming year I wish you much energy, much intellectual curiosity, much goodness of heart. The little book I'm giving you is supposed to help you understand the relationship between antiquity and Christianity. The ancient Orient (Ugarit, for instance) must not be neglected, but the most important roots of our own culture are in antiquity and Christianity. It's marvelous how Christianity synthesizes Jewish and Greco-Roman thinking. Llull's last remark in Madrid suggested that the task of our own time is to bring Christianity and Asian religions together. How fitting that you wrote about Korea in your school newspaper! —Hu Nam will tell you still more about her native land.

Your letter once again gave me great pleasure, as did, of course, your visit. Since I was not to begin my trip until that afternoon, I still had time to go to the café, which had reopened after the summer vacation. Everyone there was in high spirits; many of the philosophers were tanned, and they were all rested and relaxed. When they saw me, they shouted excitedly: "It's Nora-Vittorio—without a letter from the little philosopheress he can't come in here." I showed them your letter and then began to read it out loud. I was repeatedly interrupted, and when I read the part where you said that if everyone was un-trustworthy, no one would be prepared to help others, Immanuel Kant said: "The kid has a naturally Kantian mind. She has already understood how moral principles have to be grounded. You make a thought experiment that consists in imagining what would happen if everyone acted in accord with a given principle. If the result is impossible or undesirable, the principle is immoral."

"But how do you know what is desirable and what is not?" someone broke in.

"We can't pursue that issue just now," I said. "Nora has another problem that is bothering her, and she needs your help in understanding it. Let me read on." When I mentioned that you couldn't stand Hobbes, René cried: "The kid has good taste! I've always found him insufferable."

Mac blushed (I watched him carefully) when I came to the part where you said that you like him much better. On the other hand, that awful Hobbes exploded in ugly laughter when I read that you rejected the motto that the means justify the end. He actually shook with laughter until René finally yelled at him to please pull himself together.

"Well, well," Hobbes said, "I'd always thought people like me claimed that the end justifies the means. And Nora puts it precisely the other way around! Hahaha! And her distinction between quarreling and the use of force seems to me to split hairs. We intellectuals are just particularly strong in argumentation, and so we want to transfer the physical confrontation onto the argumentative level. It's true that it's in our interest to do so, but it still proceeds precisely from our will to power. Hahaha! If there are laws in Turkey that permit torture, they are naturally just, because the only standard of justice is the laws themselves. What are natural law theorists talking about when they say they have another standard? I don't know of any other!"

"Quiet, you monster!" Immanuel shouted. "Of course laws can be unjust, and naturally the point is that the state not be merely slavishly *feared,* but rather that its laws *recognize* our responsible, self-binding freedom."

"Self-binding freedom? That's too much for me," Hobbes cried, and whinnying with laughter, he trotted out of the café. Frankly, I was relieved to be rid of that malicious fellow. He wouldn't have been able to make any contribution to the discussion about the Trinity. After I read the philosophers your observations, you could have heard a pin drop in the café. Finally a portly, tonsured man wearing a white habit and a black coat stood up and announced:

"No one can understand the Trinity. We can only believe in it. And we must believe in it, because the Church teaches it. Anyone who does not believe will be damned."

"Now wait a minute, Thomas, that's going too fast," called out—who do you think?—our friend Llull, of course, whom I had not yet noticed and who gave me a friendly wink. "God cannot damn anyone who really tries to understand something but fails in the attempt. Precisely because God wants to be loved, but nobody can be loved who is not also known, He has to be knowable in principle. Thus the Trinity can be explained rationally . . ."

"*If* it exists," shouted al-Farabi and a man dressed as a rabbi who turned out to be Maimonides. "And conversely, if it is not rationally comprehensible, then it doesn't exist," the Islamic and Jewish philosophers continued, speaking in chorus.

"You're crazy if you grant them that," Thomas cried anxiously. "You have to appeal to your belief."

"But then they will appeal to *their* belief," Llull replied. "I can hardly expect them to be prepared to accept the superiority of my arguments if I am not myself prepared to give up my own beliefs in response to their objections."

"So, Ramon, shoot away," al-Farabi and Maimonides said. Ramon looked around the café and recognized sitting at a table in the back an elderly man with a long beard who was wearing modern Jewish clothing. "Martin, come here a minute," he called. "We're concerned with an exciting problem. My interlocutors don't regard you as suspect. Tell me, what was your most important philosophical experience?"

"The I-Thou experience. It seems to me that it is quite false to categorize it in the way that people categorize subject-object relationships.

The way I behave toward another human being is fundamentally different from the way I behave toward the natural world."

"And is this other world higher or lower than the subject-object relationship?" Llull asked, smiling surreptitiously at all three dialogue partners.

"Higher, of course!" they all answered. "Who wouldn't rather have a relationship with another person than with a stone?"

"And now tell me: should we attribute higher or lower capacities to God?"

"Higher, obviously—even the highest possible."

"But then God must not be mentally related only to an objective world, He must also possess in himself a structure of interpersonality. Otherwise he would be isolated and incapable of a relationship between subject and subject."

"What you say is well-argued," al-Farabi answered after a while, "and I have to admit that I find your line of thought rather impressive. Also, I can't yet see which of the two premises from which you derive this conclusion we have too quickly conceded. Moreover, they seem to me true, although the consequences don't appeal to me—even if I know, of course, that the consequence must be correct, *if* the premises are correct. My objection is this: aren't you Christians polytheists? Don't you believe in a plurality of Gods?"

"God forbid!" cried Llull passionately. "Of course there is only one God. But His essence is differentiated and structured. If God is one, then in Him there is a unifying element, a unified element, and the act of unifying—that is, a triune structure. And the whole world that was created by Him reflects this Trinity. You mentioned the conclusion first—doesn't it consist in two premises and a conclusion? Doesn't space have three dimensions? Doesn't time have three temporal modes, past, present, and future?"

"Wait a minute, wait a minute—you've switched lines of argument. Now you're talking about the meaning of the Trinity in the world order. Earlier you were talking about intersubjectivity. Moreover, that's a pretty new argument that I haven't yet found in your works. But intersubjectivity involves two, not three!"

"Really? Think of the family. Two people who love each other create, through their love, a new person—the child," Hegel suddenly interjected, since Llull was at a loss for words. Hegel had shortly before sat down at the table and was following the discussion with passionate interest.

"You're really subtle!" the other three laughed. "Even if we were to grant you two the Trinity (of course, we'd have to think about that for a long time, and anyway we can remind Thomas that up to this point at least we seem not to have been damned; instead, after our deaths we were assigned to this nice café, where we feel very much at our ease), Nora's objections to Jesus remain strong. There is something pagan about considering an ordinary human being divine."

"First of all, it's very important to distinguish between the immanent Trinity and the systematic Trinity," Llull replied, "that is, between the Trinity that was in God before the creation and therefore before the birth of Jesus, and the Trinity that is at work in human history. The former is already hard enough to understand, but it's easier than the latter. Moreover, you have to distinguish between the question whether an incarnation of God is a meaningful notion at all, and the question whether Jesus is God incarnate. I personally believe that the following considerations speak in favor of the Incarnation: God is infinite, and as infinite, He must create something in which He can fully express Himself. An infinite space, an infinite time—all that does not exhaust an infinite God. What it comes down to is deifying the highest being, that is, the moral human being."

"Precisely," Hegel answered, "the gulf between God and the world must be sublated. And that will happen only if something intramundane is simultaneously divine. But what is worthy of this deification? The purest human being. That He is God's son means nothing other than that the moral law is realized in Him in an unsurpassable way."

"And what does the Holy Spirit mean, then?"

"It means," Hegel continued, "that the realization of God's will in the figure of Jesus is only its beginning, not its end. On one hand, the realization of the state ruled by law, and on the other, the penetration of belief by philosophy (and of course also the history of the church) are products of the Holy Spirit. At the moment it's fluttering very powerfully among us."

"Ah, you rationalistic monster," Thomas cried in utter anguish.

"Now then," Hegel laughed, "the fact that you don't go beyond insults and don't act also shows the effect of the spirit of charity."

All these difficult discussions were making my head spin. So I was really happy to give a seminar for managers the next day—that's soberer stuff. In the meantime, I've followed in your footsteps in Liguria and soon I'll be going to Naples—a philosophical city where I'm hoping to have many encounters.

Yours, Vittorio

---

27 October 1994

Dear Vittorio,

First, thanks for the book you gave me for my birthday. I've already read some of it, and it's very interesting—that is, I like it a lot! However, I can't yet translate some of the Latin expressions. Naturally, I also enjoyed your letter very much. What subtle ideas and arguments these philosophers have! Now we've really "given it" to Hobbes. And if you ever meet him again, you can tell him that when I wrote "the means justify the end" I simply made a mistake. Naturally, what I meant was "the end justifies the means." But I can easily understand why Hobbes found that so funny, since when people are driven into a corner and are in danger of making fools of themselves, they like to look for mistakes their opponents have made.

Yes, Immanuel, I can only hope to acquire a few characteristics from you and from all the philosophers in the café. It's a good thing that Vittorio is around to put us in contact!

Dear café-philosophers: could we discuss sometime soon what is "not desirable"? That was already mentioned, and it's a stimulating subject, isn't it?

And now about the Trinity again:

Like Maimonides and al-Farabi, I don't have many objections to Llull's argument about the Trinity.

The argument is really not bad. But I also think there's something wrong with it. Do we have to attribute the same qualities to God as to human beings? Maybe God doesn't need a real subject-to-subject relationship? For God, other laws hold—not necessarily the same as those for human beings. Moreover, God can establish relationships with human beings, even if that's not the same thing; we still have something divine in us, and if God had already created such relationships in Himself, then we wouldn't need this divine element, since then we wouldn't be able to recognize God at all in order to establish such a relationship with Him. In addition, Llull contradicts himself:

First he says that the Trinity has to be conceivable for human beings, so that we can believe in it. But then he explains that God can be triune in order to establish relationships. That's pretty hard for our little human understanding to grasp, isn't it? At least I can't imagine it. How about you? You know who that reminds me of? Nicholas of Cusa. He said that in God contraries were transcended. In that respect the Trinity would be okay again: for God (or in God), one can be three . . .

Well, I don't know exactly what I should think now. I'd like not to say so much against the Trinity, since I am a Christian myself and I'm going to catechism class right now. —

Finally, my expectations have been fulfilled:

Finally I met another one of the "smart guys."

For mysterious reasons, these philosophers sometimes hang out in the neighborhood of my school. But it's probably because the train station is only ten minutes away. Well, I was on my way from school to the train station, and I was alone because I was the only passenger who had chorus, and so I'd stayed an hour later. Also, the station was almost empty, except for a man who was sitting on a bench way at the back. I sat down next to him and didn't pay any particular attention to him.

I was a little bored—I still had fifteen minutes to wait for the train—and so I took out my religion book to read a little in it (we'd been talking about Islam). But I also glanced at the chapter on Judaism. When I got to a picture that showed a rabbi, I stopped, for the man next to me said all of a sudden: "Oh—he looks like Rabbi Yitzhak!"

"Who?" I asked.

"Rabbi Yitzhak. Naturally, Nora, you're a Christian and can't know who this man is. He was an old scribe—a Jew. With his help—and that of others—I wrote my book 'Der Weg des Menschen'!"

"Martin! What a surprise! What are you doing here?"

"I'm waiting for the train. I'm going to Essen, to the famous café."

"I have to go in the same direction. That's convenient. And since we've met here, we have to use the opportunity to talk about important things," I said. "Martin, tell me about yourself and your life."

"Well, right now I'm revising my chapter 'Hier, wo man steht' again. I have to make clear to everyone interested exactly what I mean by it."

"Then try to talk to me about it, I mean, to explain it to me."

"Well, let's start. But don't hold it against me if I make a few mistakes. In my old age I don't think as clearly as I used to. Do you believe your dreams or visions?"

"Well, it depends. But probably not."

"Good. But Herr Yitzhak from Krakau (a Jew) did . . ." He told me the story of the treasure under the bridge, etc., and then he went on: "I interpreted the story this way: people should start 'digging.' Right where they're standing. That is, you mustn't wait until you get rich, for example. In every situation you should be on the lookout for something good to do, to begin finding peace. The treasure and the talents are found inside us. We don't usually have to travel to distant 'lands.' We have to travel within ourselves. With the treasure you dig up you can often bring God down to earth . . ."

"What do you mean by that?" I asked curiously.

"God allows us to draw Him into this world. When we pray to Him, believe in Him, and have begun to understand Him a little, then He is in us and around us, we have brought him down to earth. That's the only way we can unite the two worlds (God's and ours), sometime or other."

"Do you believe that Paradise will be on earth?"

"What do you think about that?"

"I believe it. Otherwise we would have no real goal on earth. Moreover, Paradise has to be comprehensible for us. Otherwise it isn't enough for humans. But then maybe we'd be angels?"

Ch-ch-ch-ch . . . Our train clattered down the tracks and stopped next to us. We got in. Martin had answered me, but I hadn't been quite able to hear what he said. In the train I'd lost the thread of our discussion and didn't bring up the question again. Unfortunately, I still had to change trains after just one station.

"See you, Martin. It was a privilege for me to discuss the subject-subject relation with you!" I called out.

"For me, too. Give Vittorio my best!"

Rum-rum-rum . . . The train moved on. I was still waving a little. — So I give you Martin's greetings, Vittorio.

At the moment I'm reading a biography of Einstein. It's really very exciting. How many theories he had! How did things go in Naples? Now you've been back for some time.

Would you sign a Greenpeace petition against the destruction and logging of the rainforest? I've already collected more than sixty signatures.

Mama and Papa are leaving tomorrow for Israel (Jerusalem). So we'll be here alone for a week. Maybe we can get together sometime.

Yours, Nora

Essen, 3 November 1994

Dear Nora,

That was a very stimulating letter—it was worth waiting so long for it. How clearly and intelligently you think—how much you read— how many interesting people you meet! I'm not at all surprised that philosophers like to hang around your school—they probably seldom find such a smart and congenial comrade. And you know, the old-man smell in the café can end up getting on your nerves—a bright young kid like you can breathe fresh life into philosophers' thoughts! It's great that you got to meet Martin Buber, but it's too bad the noise of the train pulling out interrupted your discussion of the possibility of a Paradise on earth. The subject is very important, and we should absolutely pursue it further. But first I have to tell you about my adventures in Naples, because they concern you in a very personal way and help explain why philosophers seek conversation with children.

As you surely know, Naples is an exceptionally chaotic, but also very exciting city—simultaneously crazy and brilliant. Traffic is completely unregulated (that is, people somehow manage to deal with each other, but pay no attention at all to traffic signs), there's trash all over the streets and a high crime rate—and at the same time philosophy flourishes there. In the old part of the city, through which processions occasionally make their way as they did in the Middle Ages, stands the Palazzo Serra di Cassano, in which a famous philosophical institute is located. It was founded by Gerardo Marotta, who was a wealthy lawyer and a noble patron. That was where I gave my lecture, and on the evening of your birthday I hurried, after a lively discussion of my thesis, to the marvelous San Carlo opera house, where Haydn's "Il mondo della luna" was being performed. I laughed until I cried over the human tendency to imagine all sorts of pipe-dreams and to fall into traps laid by deceivers who tell people what they want to hear. I came out of the opera house in a somewhat melancholy mood,

and walked to the Piazza Plebiscito, which is so beautifully sur-
rounded by the church's columned hall. I sat down at a little table at
the Café Gambrinus (where in our century Benedetto Croce used to
spend time) and ordered a lemon ice. Dreamily, I looked at the moon,
which seemed quite near, and asked myself what I'd like to see in it
now. Then—the man in the moon suddenly became visible and—
plunged from the moon onto our good old earth. I closed my eyes in
fear, because I was afraid he might fall on me and crush me. Nothing
happened, but when after a while I opened my eyes again, I was no
longer alone at my table. A gentleman with dark eyes and a handsome aristocratic nose was smiling at me, and it seemed I'd already
seen him somewhere. But I was so confused that I did not immediately recognize him.

"I know you'd have liked to see Nora in the moon, but she's home
in Germany celebrating her beloved grandmother's birthday. So
I've come as a substitute—allow me to introduce myself, I'm Nora's
guardian philosopher."

"Guardian philosopher?" I asked, bewildered. "What's that?"

"It's well known that ordinary children have guardian angels. But
guardian philosophers are assigned to philosophically gifted children
in order to supervise their intellectual development. You can easily
imagine that many of them have been swarming around Nora, which
is also shown by all these meetings she's had with other philosophers.
But I am Nora's true and genuine guardian philosopher, even if she
hasn't met me yet."

"What's your name?"

"You'll have to find that out for yourself. We are in Naples—a
philosophical city."

"No doubt," I said, "what Gaarder is in Oslo, De Crescenzo is
here—splendid popularizers of philosophy from the far north and the
deep south of our continent. But you wouldn't be De Crescenzo,
would you?"

"No, no," he laughed, "I'm rather the opposite type. When I
wrote my books, nobody paid any attention to me, whereas nowadays
people talk about me a lot—but things will go the other way for De
Crescenzo."

Then I went pale, because I recognized him—I had already met
him once in Rüttenscheid; moreover, I'd often seen his portrait and
his statue. But Haydn's music had made me blind to what was right in
front of my eyes.

"Giambattista!" I cried, "forgive your translator for the sake of his labors on your work! I'm terribly embarrassed not to have recognized you at once. And I'm so happy that it's you who are Nora's guardian philosopher."

"I am too," he laughed, "because I was one of the first to take an interest in children—that is, in their own ways of thinking and feeling. For that reason it was natural that I be chosen—Jean-Jacques was also a possibility, but his candidacy was severely damaged by Nora's acute observation that true friends of children didn't put their own children in orphanages. I, on the contrary, wrote "The New Science" while my children were tugging on my legs."

"I know, Giambattista, and that always impressed me very much. I couldn't have imagined a better guardian philosopher for Nora."

"Thanks, thanks. But alongside my personal inclination toward children, another factor in my appointment was that I combined a research program with my guardianship. As you know, I start out from the fact that the whole human race and the individual develop in parallel: in earlier ages, imagination and feelings were stronger, as they are nowadays in each child; in later ages and among adults they are restricted by the understanding. The poetic vitality and sweep of a poet like Homer is denied a rational age like ours, and when Nora is thirty years old even she will no longer write so spontaneously as she does now. Secondly, I am of the opinion that while the development toward an increasingly dominant role for reason is on the whole a good one, there is a danger that an emotionally arid kind of thinking could lead to barbarous reflection, that is, to reasoning without belief in the truth, an egotistical, calculating falsity, and an irresponsible, officious meddling. That sort of thing destroyed ancient Rome, and it endangers modern Europe. Regeneration can be brought about through the naive and intelligent goodness of children and simple cultures. For example, I find it exceptionally important that Nora has worked in support of the Brazilian native populations and their rainforest—since the children of the age of the triumph of modern science will be most strongly affected by it, they must also begin to defend themselves as soon as possible! I also find it very important that Nora is interested not only in present and future problems, but also in ancient cultures. Paradoxically, we can oppose the dangerous tendencies of our time only if we are acquainted with the spiritual treasures of our past. For instance, a person familiar with classical culture finds it easier to see what is dangerous in our world—for example, the high status accorded to the infinite at the expense of the sense of limits and proportions."

"Very true," I replied, "and therefore I hope Nora will also learn Greek."

"Speaking of Greek, here we are in Greater Greece, and at night ancient Greece comes back to life in 'New City'—it was called 'Neapolis' in Greek. Do you know Posillipo?"

"How could I not know it? While I was translating you, I lived for a considerable time on that beautiful headland, where Virgil's villa also stood."

"'Posillipo' comes from Greek *pausilupos,* 'where pain comes to an end.' Today a splendid party is being held there, and we should make an appearance at it."

"Are we invited?"

"Of course," Giambattista smiled mysteriously, "Nora's guardian philosopher and her pen pal must not fail to be there."

He beckoned to a taxi, and we climbed in, but I was astonished to notice that the driver was dressed not like a modern Neapolitan but like a Greek. He grinned at me and said: "Today it's not horses but a motor that carries me there, even if not in so natural a way as earlier."

"My dear Parmenides," Giambattista answered, "so then you acknowledge that time exists, since you speak of 'earlier.' I thought you accepted only pure being without becoming."

"After I read you, I revised my opinions. But Albert avenged me— since everything is determined, everything later is contained in every point in time, and so time is an illusion after all."

Whether it is an illusion or not, we soon arrived in Posillipo. And in a broad meadow on top of the cliffs, with a splendid view of Capri, a large number of people were standing—almost the whole group from the Rüttenscheid café and more besides. They held glasses of water in their hands (only one of them was holding the water in his hand itself, and that was naturally Diogenes), and as we got out of the taxi they all sang in chorus: "Happy birthday, dear Nora!"

When they had finished, Heraclitus said to Parmenides: "You know, everything changes, and time is the true power. But it's marvelous to act as though we could stop it, and have an enduring experience of the finest moments—of course, afterward we notice with a jolt that we've grown older and that time really does determine everything."

"And yet it is an illusion," Parmenides murmured, but he understood that it wasn't the moment to disturb the party mood by engaging in a philosophical controversy . . .

Dear Nora, I hope this report will bring you still more happiness for your next year!

Yours, Vittorio

------

27 November 1994

Dear Vittorio,

I enjoyed your letter very much again. It was really beautiful, but also instructive, since I learned only by accident that Giambattista is my guardian philosopher! And now we also know where the office of guardian philosophers is located. It is obviously on the moon, since Giambattista came from the moon to visit you. Maybe you will someday be on the moon too, available for service as a guardian philosopher!

Too bad, I would have so much liked to attend my birthday party. I would have brought a cake (because we both especially like cake). I must ask Giambattista sometime if he likes cakes too. I think he does.

Now, on birthdays Diogenes ought to drink from a glass. Otherwise, celebrations are nothing special for him. —You know, drivers in Naples don't really exemplify Hobbes's maxim that "man is a wolf to man," because there people can get along without traffic signs (laws). People aren't so dumb after all!

The development of human beings is parallel to the development of history, that's . . . actually true. An example is belief in gods. People thought up imaginative gods that were appropriate for them and that they could explain to themselves. That's a kind of childish belief. The belief in one God is a step forward in reason, that is, like becoming more mature and intelligent, more adult. And I like the way Giambattista says that we should concern ourselves more with the problems of humanity and the earth rather than always trying to find God or explain Him. Although it is very tempting to do so.

So what does he mean, anyway, when he says that Europe is in danger? According to Hegel everything tends toward the good, and humanity repeatedly takes small steps forward. Now and then people also confront certain dangers and accidents, but we still learn something new from them and gradually move toward the truth. And Western Europe is on the path toward unity! That is truly progress. And for just that reason all the people who live there are called upon not to just revolve around themselves but to get acquainted with the newly reopened European countries and to think about them. I'm inclined to believe that Europe is on the rise again, or soon will be. We are a model for other countries and continents. Unfortunately the former Yugoslavia is still there! But it is also part of Europe. Maybe we could try, as a united Europe, to put an end to the conflict there—maybe.

So, to turn now to the subject of "Paradise on earth," which is also part of the progress of humanity: I believe, at least at the moment, that this earthly paradise will come into existence. Because: (a) Paradise must be for us human beings, and therefore we must be able to conceive it, and (b) what would be the point of creating earth if the Garden of Eden doesn't come here? We human beings must have once been able to make good triumph and to act in accord with it. If we didn't need to fight for the good and the divine that are in us they would be essentially superfluous. And we do know, after all, that good must triumph in the world! This knowledge would be superfluous if we didn't act in accord with it. We also want everything to be good someday. First we have to succeed in building Paradise on earth, and then, when God has seen that we are ready for it, he will bring us into the world of souls, and there eternity begins! I believe that we will be able to do this. But do you know what occurs to me just now? In Paradise, what happens to people who have been bad and who are also not contrite? Do you believe in the Last Judgment? I'm not so sure.—

I'll have to really think about the question as to whether time is an illusion. What occurs to me first is that it really isn't important for human beings to know whether time is an illusion or not. What difference would it make to us to know that it is an illusion, for example? We couldn't do anything with that knowledge, because *we* still have to go on living in time and space. On the other hand, it would be exciting, of course, to discover the secret of time! I find Parmenides' view subtle. It is true that nothing can come from nothing. But maybe God played a role here. And I believe that for sure.—

I'm reading the Nibelungen saga right now. Earlier I read two good chivalric romances—Parsifal and Gudrun. The Middle Ages is really stimulating!

Bye, Nora

P.S. Hope to see you soon!

Dear Nora,

The club just about flipped out when, immediately after class, I came into the café waving your latest letter—for which I thank you very much. I had not been there for a relatively long time, and the philosophers were waiting impatiently for news about you. Most of them had heard about Giambattista's being named your guardian philosopher, and I can tell you that the poor man now has to put up with lots of jealousy—the position was much desired. Jean-Jacques snubbed Giambattista for a month, and Tom constantly teases him, asking whether he has grown wings yet—true guardian philosophers must begin to look like guardian angels as well. Oh, well, even philosophers are human-all-too-human. I was moreover very happy that you think I might someday become a guardian philosopher. I could hardly imagine a more wonderful task after death—it's just too bad that you will then be too big for me to be assigned to you. (Anyway, if I live a few years longer, as I hope to do, my dream-job in the beyond is already occupied.)

Your observation regarding Neapolitan drivers was immediately picked up. An elegant American named Lawrence, about whom it is said that he was allowed to come to the café only at the invitation of one of the philosophers, because he really did something different, called out: "The girl is really smart! She understands that life with laws and rules is only one possibility—mutual give and take (for example, yielding the right of way) is also a solution to social problems. If she brings this idea into connection with the concept of development, she'll see that in the development of the individual as in the development of the species, law-and-order morality is a later stage than mere reciprocity. However, I must admit that this kid has made me uneasy again. Because I find her such a fascinating conversation partner, as a research-object she would make me very insecure. She philosophizes in a way that should not yet occur in children of this age, according to my theory. Thus: either my theory is false, or this Nora does not exist."

Here Tom laughed out loud and cried: "It's far more likely that you don't exist—and for that matter, all of us! In any case, most adults think that, whereas Nora's youth is shown precisely by her belief in everything Vittorio tells her. I'll bet she still believes in Father Christmas!"

Just then the door opened, and Father Christmas came in! Tom's jaw dropped, he was so surprised.

"Hey, Tom," René called out, "that shuts you up, doesn't it? Now you feel yourself contradicted. But the contradiction involved in arguing against your own existence is still more flagrant, even if you hardly noticed it. When will you finally learn to reflect on yourself?"

In the meantime, Father Christmas had taken off his beard—it was a false one—and people recognized him: it was Diogenes of Sinope. "Children, children," he sighed, "it may be that I exaggerated a little—but the consumerism of *this* society borders on insanity. I was just in a big department store, where I disguised myself as Father Christmas in order to get a closer look at this buying madness. It was dreadful how many children have fallen victim to it—all the stuff they want to have, and always with the same argument, that their classmates get that much. Whether it's stereos, Walkmen, or cell phones—it just goes on and on. And how much they love CD-players! Good old Plato was right in one respect: the media affect the message very significantly. The book has really suppressed true dialogue, and the CD-player makes it no longer necessary to prepare yourself as a complete person to listen to music. Earlier, one could hear Bach's St. Matthew's Passion only during Holy Week—only after Lent, after cleansing the body and purifying the soul, was one allowed access to this work of art. These days, anyone can listen to a few measures while eating breakfast or reading the paper or browsing in a music store, and then shut the CD-player off again."

"And what especially struck me," Augustine said, shaking his head, "is that this buying frenzy is almost the only thing left of the celebration of Christmas. In our time, Christianity freed itself from the trappings of hedonism—whereas today it has dwindled into gifts and their wrappings."

"I wonder whether Europe will really succeed in solving its problems and especially in restraining its standard of living?" asked a man with a strong Swiss accent. (His accent made him stand out in the club, because not many Swiss belonged to it). "After the horrors of the twentieth century, Hegel's optimistic view of progress seems unbearably naive!"

"Now, Jakob," Immanuel said, "you may criticize Hegel, but children have to give us courage, and your pessimism only makes the situation worse. Your prophecies become self-fulfilling—if people no longer have hope, they don't try anymore. But we should be alert to all the dangers that threaten us, and in particular we must recognize that not everything we actually want is worth having. I believe that the finest Christmas gift we can give is to limit our wishes to what is worth having. We shouldn't get everything we want; instead, we should want to have the right wishes—and that also means that we should want to be happy and satisfied with little. A more modest way of life is the most valuable thing that we can receive."

"Isn't it strange that today humanity is threatened not primarily by wars and diseases—at least not humanity here in Western Europe—but rather by their own technological successes, which can become disastrous?" asked a voice that seemed familiar. I looked over—and it was Hans Jonas.

"You, here?" I asked in surprise.

"Where else?" he replied with a friendly smile. "Though I must tell your little friend that that Paradise on earth stuff is not without its dangers. I think it's good that Nora has worked on behalf of justice, but unfortunately the battle for the good can easily slip over into horror—just think of the communist experiment. How pathetically that project failed!"

"Yes, my namesake," said a somber and gloomy-looking gentleman whom I immediately took for a Spaniard, "that's what happens when you forget sinfulness."

"Nothing straight and true can come out of such rotten wood," Immanuel cackled.

"Yes," the Spaniard went on, "and if people have a presumptuous, excessively lofty view of themselves, they may think they can make earth a Paradise, and then they may easily end up making it a Hell. The meaning of life consists in our fighting for the good—but we cannot completely eliminate evil from this world. For that someone else is needed."

"And is Hell part of this other world?" I asked. "Nora has to know."

"Not now or ever," cried a man with a massive chest and a rather high voice. "How could that be reconciled with God's goodness?"

"Oh, Origen," Augustine broke in, "when will you abandon your heresy?"

"Listen here, Augustine, if you had your way I'd already be broiling in Hell. Instead, I'm in the café and feel very happy here. Thus there is no Hell."

"Okay, for you there is none—I was hasty in consigning you to it. But you are hasty when you assume that no one is in Hell. Where else would real villains (not charming heretics with whom I've come to enjoy talking—this café is so pleasant) be?"

"Don't you have any sympathy for them? Especially if God has predestined them to be evil, he cannot finally damn them, but only send them to Purgatory."

"Here we are back at the problem of freedom! But Christmas is coming up, and we don't want to start fighting now; instead, let's just ask Nora whether she thinks Judas is in Hell or not."

Well, dear Nora, this question is bothering everybody in the club! They need help! Please write soon!

Yours, Vittorio

-----

23 December 1994

Dear Vittorio,

Unfortunately, I wasn't able to write a proper answer to your letter. This is sort of an in-between letter. Also, your Christmas gift is not quite ready. I'm really very sorry. But your letter was so beautiful and instructive! I no longer want a CD-player so much, but that also comes from having met Diogenes. (Disguised as Father Christmas, he was looking with desire and fascination at a CD-player—while he was eating Gummi-Bears!) He is visiting me again. Do you think that in our own time Diogenes would still have lived in a barrel? I don't!

Regarding Paradise on earth: if people's search for freedom ends up making a Hell, then they have not correctly understood peace and humanity. I believe that there will also be a Paradise on earth. When we have gotten far enough, then the Kingdom of Heaven can come.

To Hobbes: Dear Hobbes, I believe in Mother Christmas! With their joy, people themselves emanate a heavenly spirit that can often be felt. Or don't you feel the mysteries that hang in the air? Mother Christmas is not a bodily figure, she is the spirit of Christmas, and if you celebrate Christmas the right way and take joy in it, then she is there. But unfortunately she doesn't seem to come to your place, otherwise you probably wouldn't find it so odd that people believe in Christmas spirits! Moreover, Mother Christmas doesn't give out gifts, but rather joy and spirit! —Merry Christmas, Nora.

Vittorio, when you run into Hobbes, would you please give him this little letter? Yesterday I had to direct our nativity play. But I also played a part: I was an innkeeper. We got the text from Hotti. It was very beautiful. How are you and your parents? Fine, I hope! Everything here is going well, and we are looking forward to tomorrow evening. In the end, I wished for books, piano music, and maybe a camera. We'll see whether I get any of those. I'm sitting here at the table, looking out the window. Soon it will be dark. Today we had our first frost. Did you have frost too? Yesterday we went to the Christmas oratorio. It was great! During the last chorale I looked up at the Cross, and it seemed to me that Jesus was smiling. I hope He was! I wish you and your family a very merry Christmas and a happy New Year. (Mama, papa, grandmother, and Bettina do too.)

Yours, Nora

P.S. I'm glad you liked the opera.

Poem

Michelangelo said his sculptures
just had to be
freed from superfluous stone.
Can't the same be said of men?
Many people are unhewn.
Nonetheless, a rough block
Does not always produce a rough wedge.

Don't you hear the drummer
beating stubbornly within you,
leading you, despite all resistance,
through the enemy camp?
Listen: he's telling you something:
when nothing excites us anymore,
that's a sign that
nothing is moving anymore.

Introversion has become fashionable,
people listen to themselves and are moved.
It's odd how they become so refined inwardly,
But often become petrified outwardly.
Still you stand at the beginning, and don't know where to go—
Yet direction is offered you.

Don't you hear the drummer . . .

HEART

(*Hermann van Veen, H. Sacksioni, R. Chrispijin, T. Vaitkewitch*)

I liked this poem so much, especially now at Christmas time. I got it from a priest.

Christmas, 1994

Dear Nora,

Your lovely letter came right on time, on Christmas eve. I was very glad to get it, and immediately read it to my parents and sisters, who also thought it was very Christmasy. I found it particularly appropriate that you told Hobbes you believed in Mother Christmas—I assume that cynic is still a male chauvinist. I haven't yet run into him here in Regensburg; he's probably hiding out somewhere these days. If I do run into him, I'll offer him a couple of Gummi-Bears—I like them a lot. Many thanks! Don't worry that your gift won't be ready on time—it's the thought that counts, and anyway we'll see each other at the beginning of January.

How was Christmas at your house? I hope it was very nice. We had a pleasant evening, with only a few presents, thank God, but with much Christmas spirit. Today I attended high mass in our Gothic cathedral: the world-famous Regensburg children's choir sang most delightfully; and as the lamps were extinguished and "Holy Night" rang out, the splendid church, the magnificent altar with its nave and two aisles, ancient stained-glass windows, and beautiful sculptures of the smiling angel of the Annunciation and the bewildered Mary (who nonetheless understood the message given her), seemed to dissolve into another tonality. The correspondences between colors and tones are remarkable. Doesn't it sometimes seem to you that colors turn into sounds and voices seem to take on colors? There seems to be a mysterious connection between individual sense impressions. Only the sermon was not outstanding—the prologue to the Gospel according to St. John is a hard act to follow. Clerics are often quick to politicize things; it is important to show that Christianity's demands extend into all the domains of human life, including politics, but if one wants to give sound advice, one also has to have a knowledge of the social sciences. Of course, for Catholics the sermon is not so important, and one is drawn into the feeling and spirit anyway when one experiences such a splendid high mass.

It therefore seems to me entirely reasonable for the Church to try to include the nonrational aspects of humanity; if they are excluded, they take their revenge. As always, on my way home I went through the Bismarckplatz. There I noticed a man in a white Dominican habit, who was hurrying barefooted toward the Dominican church. "Well, now," I thought, "that is not Diogenes' barrel, but given these temperatures, he must be cold. I should give him the pair of stockings I got for Christmas."

I went up to him and said: "Father, you're going to get cold."

"Don't worry, I'm used to it," he answered. "Really cold weather keeps me young—in fact, too young," he said, winking.

I stared at the gaunt man, who somehow seemed familiar. The association I had led to my school days. Was he one of my former teachers? I smiled in a bewildered way and acted as though I knew exactly who he was.

"Ah, it's nice to see you again. Have you retired in the meantime? Or are you still teaching?"

"I never stop teaching—anything that stands outside my teaching is not truly mine. But I've long since ceased to serve as bishop here—I'm free of that obligation."

Bishop? No bishop had ever taught in my school. I wondered whether the man was mad. Then he winked at me again and said: "Winking is not a mere tic that you've often experienced. On the contrary, you've never seen me wink. Every day and night you've seen me looking into being with open eyes."

Then *I* was almost turned to stone: it was Albertus Magnus, formerly bishop of Regensburg, whose statue I had passed a thousand times on the way out of my school.

"Forgive me, Albert, for not immediately recognizing you!"

"Well," he said, "I've forgiven graver offenses, and not only at Christmas time. Don't worry, people recognize only those who correspond to their expectations, and I admit that my appearance may be somewhat surprising."

"To tell the truth, as a philosopher I ought to be used to surprises. The sense of wonder is, after all, our distinguishing mark. All the same, I'm happy to meet you. It's too bad that you didn't give the sermon in the cathedral today."

"In exchange, you can participate in a religious discussion. I have an appointment to meet . . ."

"Maimonides or al-Farabi?"

"No, that would be too easy. Today I'm speaking with Lao-tzu. He is waiting in the church. Come along."

We went into a church much smaller than the cathedral, where an Asian man approached us with a broad smile.

"So, Albert, did you bring a friend along to the debate? You Westerners, who constantly want to discuss matters! A little while ago I saw your nativity scene in front of the altar, and I thought about the relationship between the Tao and this newborn child. In the end, I wasn't sure whether I was Lao-tzu, looking at the child Jesus, or Jesus, smiling at Lao-tzu."

"Yes, we have a different relation to the active life than you do, Lao-tzu. If you only knew how many organizational tasks I had to assume as bishop! They prevented me from engaging in contemplation, but it is also our duty to serve justice, and we can do that only if we act, manage, and organize."

"I, on the other hand, adhere to Wu-Wei, the principle of doing nothing," Lao-tzu replied with a smile. "The great man does nothing, he has an effect. He radiates his unity with the Tao, and so he doesn't need to organize anything."

"I also find the influence of a great personality overpowering— that's why we celebrate Christmas."

"You, perhaps; but you are eternally young, yet you are already dead—not so long as I have been, true, but still a good seven hundred years. However, when I go through the festively lit streets and shops of your city and observe people frantically scurrying about in search of presents, I have my doubts as to whether many people still feel the Child's influence. If Westerners only used their organizational skills to alleviate need—but often as not they use them to exploit need. Say, Albert, I've got a question for you that has concerned me for a long time: your Christian theologians have striven mightily to prove by argumentation that Christianity is superior to other religions."

"Yes, for unlike other religions ours is based on Greek philosophy. Our religion was related to the *logos* from the outset—the Child is the *logos* incarnate."

"That may well be, but do you find Europe's current situation really so attractive?"

"No, no," Albert replied, shaking his head, "I find it truly deplorable. This materialism has led us so far away from Christianity's roots. My friends from the café who went through the historicist school tell me that even between our medieval conception of Christianity and early Christianity the gap was very large. But the gap between the latter and the modern world is enormous."

"Precisely. And now for my question: how is it that your culture, which is so proud of its religion and has always seen itself as the apex of human development, has produced a society dominated by so many petty hucksters and consumers? Only in the West is atheism a mass phenomenon—and in my own country, in China, it is the result of Western imports. How can an atheistic society have developed on a Christian foundation?"

"Ah," sighed Albert, "if only I could answer your question! For a time, it seemed to me that when at the beginning of the modern age Christianity spread all over the world as a result of colonization, its triumph was about to be achieved. Today I am often upset to see the conception of Christian-European culture the mass media have put into everyone's heads. Environmental destruction concerns me very much."

"Well, you Christians have separated God from nature far too much."

"No, Lao-tzu, that can't be it. I also consider nature to penetrated by God through and through, and so far as I'm concerned it is divine— though not identical with God. Anyone who identifies the two robs humanity of the possibility of raising itself toward God, that is, above nature. God is not nature, as you seem to believe, nor is the relation-ship between God and nature arbitrary, as some theologians who came after me assumed. God's reason is manifested in the ordering of nature, but goes beyond it."

"Yes, but it is precisely because you Europeans don't see yourselves as part of nature that you feel the need to transform everything, change things, and not accept anything the way it is."

"To be sure, but we really have to change many things. Should we remain silent when confronted by injustices? Shouldn't we strive to improve people's lives on earth?"

"Oh, yes, we should help everyone to have a fulfilling life and to grow old. But when the basic needs are met, then we should know how to call a halt. And your culture has proven incapable of doing that."

"Once again, your criticism is correct. But I find it remarkable and incomprehensible that the current situation has grown out of Chris-tianity. Precisely because for us Christians, God also manifests Him-self in history, I am confronted by an insoluble question: What are God's plans in this epoch of history—an epoch that could be titled 'The Dissolution of Christendom'?"

"Could it be that Christianity's crisis should lead it to become humbler? It should recognize that God reveals Himself in other religions as well, and that some new arrangement has to be worked out that will allow people to live together in peace. In any case it is a great step forward that you no longer regard me as a simple heathen but are willing to discuss matters with me."

"Yes," Albert replied with a smile, "that might be an answer. But much remains that is enigmatic and mysterious."

"Thank God! Wouldn't it be boring if all mysteries were resolved? On one hand I feel sorry for people who have to live today and cannot simply move through the world as observers, as we do, at most sitting in cafes talking with girls and young professors who listen to us. On the other hand, I envy them, because this is an extraordinarily exciting time to live in, and the confrontation between our cultures seems to be one of the chief tasks facing humanity today. Alongside all the superficialities that currently bedevil us, alongside all the horrible conflicts that are being waged between different cultures, there is also the hope that from the encounter between differing cultures something enduring might emerge."

"Yes, our religion also has its source in the encounter between Judaism and Greek thought—an encounter that stretched over many centuries and eventually sought to reconcile Aristotle as well as Plato with Christianity . . ."

"And we all know that was your achievement, dear Albert! Will there be another Albert who can unite Asian thought with Christianity?"

"Well, we must ask the help of the small Child in the manger."

And both of them turned to the Child Jesus, who was smiling sweetly between an ox and an ass. It warmed my heart, despite the cold in the unheated church, and after a while I returned home.

Wasn't that a wonderful Christmas encounter? Dear Nora, I wish you a happy New Year, with much joy, creative power, and insight.

Yours, Vittorio

———————

3 January 1995

Dear Vittorio,

Thanks so much for your letter; it was truly a Christmas letter, and not only because of your meeting with Albertus Magnus and Lao-tzu in the little church!

Right now I'm sitting in a cozy little room in my aunt's house, in Sauerland. It's already dark outside, but the snow still glistens a little. Imagine—the snow is almost a meter deep. And it has fallen since we've been here, that is, since Saturday. We came here to rest up a bit, because Mama, Bettina, and I got a cold, and my nose is still stopped up. But I'm already feeling better.

Christmas was very nice here, too. Our preacher gave a good sermon, and at the end all the lights were shut off except for the ones on the Christmas tree, and then we bellowed out the hymn "O du fröhliche." That made us all feel very festive. Afterward we looked at the nativity scene again (ours is very beautiful), and then walked home in our boots through the cold. When we got home, we drank tea while we listened to a story Mama read aloud. At about seven, we sang lots of Christmas carols again, and then the clock in Mama's workroom struck: and—really—the door swung open and we were astonished to see a lovely Christmas tree. The presents were lying all around it. Oh, Vittorio, although I no longer wanted a CD-player, and had told Papa and Mama so, I got one anyway! And it turns out to be not so bad, on the contrary. But I also got books and a new bed. (In addition, I got something from Grandma, Grandfather, and all my aunts and uncles, but that's not so important now.) And then you gave us the opera tickets as well! Many, many thanks.

We also had a great celebration on New Year's eve up here in Sauerland. I hope you did too. I'm looking forward to the new year (and it has already gotten off to a good start). I hope Christmas remains in peoples' hearts and accompanies them through the new year.

Now for Albertus's and Lao-tzu's concerns and questions:

It's really not easy to say why an atheistic and egoistic society developed on a Christian foundation. I believe that this kind of society developed because:

1. Christianity is not very closely connected with everyday life, at least not these days. For that reason many people simply forget that there is a God, because they are not constantly reminded of Him by certain daily rituals, as they are in Islam, for instance.

2. Humanity has made a great effort to understand, and we can now know, how the earth emerged, namely through the Big Bang, how everything developed and how everything is related regarding life and natural forces. And many people may no longer be able to imagine God the creator who made and produced all this, but instead

they believe that everything can be explained in strictly scientific terms and that the earth's emergence is an accident.

3. Because Christianity puts special emphasis on the individual and sets him above nature, and, as it also says in the Bible, regards him as the lord of the earth, many people elevate themselves to divine status!

You know, they also asked what God's plans for this technological age might be; I think that God has no direct plans for us at all, only a wish. God has put the world in our hands, so that we might undertake the difficult task of making it into a human paradise. He has given us the world, so to speak, and can't really determine anything here on earth. He can only help us, when we "call" Him.

And so we have to find a way of making the present age better, all by ourselves—God is with us, but doesn't direct anything Himself.

One way could be to join forces with the Asian world and its religions. That would be good, because then maybe busy, ambitious striving and working just to earn money among people here in Europe would subside a bit, because people would keep more in touch with Wu-Wei, with doing nothing. Maybe a new religion would even develop, the way Christianity once developed out of Greek, Hellenistic, and Jewish religion. This time it would develop out of Christian and Asian thinking. Along with a new religion come wars (probably), because every religion has orthodox members who don't want a new one. Moreover, Asian thought includes not only Confucianism and Taoism, but also Buddhism and Hinduism, and those are still religions with many gods. And I wonder whether it will be so easy to combine Christianity with polytheism . . . —

You also discussed Europe's—and therefore Christianity's—activity and urge to do research. If I remember correctly, Albertus and Lao-tzu found this technological progress cause for concern. But I understand them only halfway. I understand them if they mean that people should direct their research more toward helping poor people, rather than constantly inventing new machines and media for Europe, which is already so rich, and thereby also causing environmental catastrophes.

But I think that activity in the sense of research and discovery is basically very good! If people had not also discovered technological things, we would still be Stone-Age hunters and gatherers. And it would also be very boring not to investigate anything. We have a certain curiosity in us with which we discover good as well as bad things. I think activity should not be banned, but we should know what we are working for. Thus we should not hang our heads, but rather become all the more active in order to change many things and use them for better things.—

Diogenes visited me again. I think he was not so angry that I had gotten a CD-player. I offered him a cup of tea, but he still wanted just water. And he taught me how to drink out of my hand.

At the moment I'm reading a biography of Friederike Caroline Neuber, who was a famous theatrical manager in the eighteenth century.

So now we are going to the opera in your city!

See you soon, Nora

Essen, 11 January 1995

Dear Nora,

As you yourself have seen, your letter was once again a great joy for me—and Albert and Lao-tzu would have enjoyed it too, had I met them again and been able to show it to them. That was, of course, my intention, but in the meantime something very remarkable happened. Yesterday, when I hurried to the café, waving your letter, *I no longer found it there.* I wandered around the neighborhood, annoyed and even desperate, and suddenly saw three men sitting on a bench.

"Excuse me," I said, "I must have gotten lost, because I can't find the Café of the Dead but Ever Young Philosophers, which must be somewhere nearby. Would you happen to know how I could get there?"

The three men roared with laughter at my politely formulated question. I found this unfriendly, and looked at the trio a little more closely. One of them wore clothes from late antiquity, the second a kilt, and the third an elegant suit, which looked to me as though it had been made around the turn of the century. Though they were dressed quite differently, their facial expressions had something in common—something pained on one hand, and merry on the other.

"The flies have finally found the way out of the bottle," said the man in the elegant suit, who had a strong Austrian accent.

"No, it's worse than that, Ludwig. The café has ceased to exist, and not for any particular reason."

"How so?" I interrupted, extremely irritated. "Changes always have a cause; something can't disappear on me just like that."

"You think so? Why?"

"Well, wouldn't you be surprised if one morning the sun didn't come up?"

"I probably couldn't be surprised, because then all life would cease. But granting that I would be surprised, if I were still alive— in fact, I would be surprised, because of the violation of a habit of which I'd become fond. But then I would say to myself: 'From the fact that the sun has so far come up, it does not logically follow that it has to come up in the future as well.'"

"That may be correct," I replied. "But one can rely on experience anyway!"

"Experience?" he laughed. "We don't have any experience of the future! *Up to now* your experience has been that the sun comes up every morning. But you have not yet been able to have the experience that the sun will come up tomorrow as well. How can you already anticipate tomorrow morning's experiences?

"Okay, so maybe I can't really exclude the possibility that tonight a cosmic catastrophe might occur and destroy the sun, but this destruction has to have a cause. It must take place in accord with natural laws."

"Natural laws? Who says there are natural laws? Do you mean by that something enduring over time?"

"Of course."

"Then we encounter the same problem again. There is not the slightest ground for assuming that what we currently hold to be natural laws will still be in force tomorrow. Natural laws could be dissolved just like your café with all its wretched flies."

"But if you don't assume a stable future, how can you make plans at all? You might just as well jump out of the window of a high-rise building as take an elevator, if it is equally probable that the usual laws of gravity will hold and that they will not. That seems to me a strong argument in favor of our belief in the stability of natural laws."

"Argument?" broke in the learned man of late antiquity. "Are there really arguments for and against a position?"

"Surely you don't think there aren't?"

"Listen: every argument is based on an assumption."

"I'll accept that."

"Either this assumption is posited without argument, or it is arbitrary, and we can just as well posit a counter-assumption. Or else you argue for this assumption. But then you need a further assumption, which has itself to be argued for, and so on, ad infinitum. Or you prove one assumption by means of another, and the latter by means of the first: then you're involved in circular reasoning, and with that you can prove anything. Therefore: there are no truly rigorous arguments. Moreover: you have to have a criterion to distinguish good arguments from bad. But you need arguments in order to legitimate the criterion. In short: you are moving hopelessly in a circle."

"I'm not sure I've understood . . ."

"And I, on the contrary, am quite sure that you have not understood him," the man with an Austrian accent broke in. "You've merely 'quunderstood' him."

"What did you say?"

"Here's what I mean: you know what addition is?"

"Sure."

"Have you ever carried out the operation on all numbers?"

"That's impossible. I am a finite being and live only in finite time."

"Good. Let's assume you've never added up two numbers that are both greater than 100,000. It is compatible with all the additions you've thus far performed that you suddenly say: "101,000 + 103,000 = 5." That is because in fact you have understood addition to be a quaddition, and the latter is defined this way: for numbers less than 100,000 it is like normal addition, and for numbers larger than 100,000 the result is always 5."

"I've really quunderstood you here—you're clowning around, the way my friend Nora, Dinosaur-Nora, does when she's in a good mood."

"I'm being serious."

"You presumably mean quserious." If you're right (oops, sorry, quright), then there is no longer any stable meaning, and then we can hardly understand each other."

"Not so fast—I just do what other people do."

"Precisely!" cried the man in the kilt, "I follow the habits I like. It's simply customary to believe in the law of gravity and to perform additions instead of quaddings. But nothing is more profound than the inertia of our nature."

"Everything is customs, everything is habits," the trio suddenly sang in chorus.

"You're a quinfernal trio!" I cried out. "I think you don't exist at all, but rather only quexist."

I had hardly said that than the three of them disappeared without a trace! And at the end of the street I recognized—the café I'd been looking for! Unfortunately, it was too late to go in, because I still had another appointment, and the conversation with the trio had eaten up a lot of time. Moreover, I was so exhausted that I no longer had the strength to engage in demanding discussions.

What do you think of these three oddballs' claims, Nora? Sometimes it seems to me that they have something important to say, and sometimes I think they're prize jokesters. What do you think?

I'm sorry that I have to begin the new year with such a strange letter, but unfortunately it's the truth about what happened to me—and I have a duty to tell you the truth, nothing but the truth.

Dear Nora, warmest greetings

from
your
Vittorio

———————

11 February 1995

Dear Vittorio,

Many thanks for your funny and peculiar letter. You know, it really confused me, and sometimes I no longer knew what to think! That's also why I've not written in such a long time. I can truly imagine the pained expression on the faces of the three "oddballs": I think that without a truth that one can find and honor, life would be sadder and perhaps more meaningless. And also so "arid"! It would be very boring without something that one can find out, don't you think? Now you have probably already noticed that I think that there is a truth. I believe that it is the eternal ideas or God. I believe that mathematics is a good example of it: Thales did not invent his theorem about the circle, he discovered it! That means that human beings can only "execute" or combine the eternal ideas when, for example, they make up stories, paint pictures, and so on. But then we would still not be completely free from fate, because we could always only discover something composed of the shadows of the eternal ideas. Isn't that right? I'm not sure.

Oh, yes, the proposition "There is no truth" is self-contradictory: if nothing is true, then this proposition cannot be true either. And then everything turns in a circle.

Vittorio, what was the real reason you didn't find the café? Were you perhaps so confused by the three men that you were won over to their view yourself?

If so, then I can easily understand it! But finally you did regain your footing, didn't you? You realized again that there is a truth, right? Because there was the café again right where it was supposed to be!

The three men did a pretty good job of confusing the world—and you and me too! It's too bad that they produced such an effect, because that could be one reason why there are so many atheists in our time—because if you don't believe in any truth, you don't believe in God!

But you said that sometimes you think the three of them had something important to say. What do you mean by that?

When I'd thought it over a bit, this is what I decided: Maybe we have to listen to them to the extent that we have to be critical and not simply assume everything without question, just as it is (that the sun comes up, that we are living, that the earth goes around the sun, etc.). But I think "things" have causes—that's clear! Because if there are eternal ideas, then they are naturally the causes. Their "consequences" will be carried out in space and time. (Human beings are so created that they always look for an event's cause. This distinguishes them from animals and plants. And I believe that there are really causes, because if human beings can imagine causes, that is proof that they exist.) What did Ludwig mean, anyway, when he said, "The flies have found the way out of the bottle"? Did he mean that philosophers, who are always seeking a way out of their problems, had finally found an exit and now know that there are no natural laws, etc.? What did he mean? Do you know? I'm going to look in the dictionary again.

At the moment I'm very interested in the Renaissance! That must have been a wonderful time. That was when exciting philosophers like Descartes appeared. Do you know what happened to me recently, a couple of days ago? I'll tell you:

I was taking a walk in the woods and was delighted to see how many flowers were already in bloom (for example, snowdrops, daffodils . . .). Birds were twittering, and the trees were already in bud. Everything was a soft green, rays of sunshine were filtering down through the tree boughs and reflecting off small ponds. I walked along and wondered at everything. Then I suddenly saw a dark-haired man sitting on a stump and looking with fascination at some snowdrops. Sitting there, the man seemed to me to have something magical about him, and I sat down—because I was tired anyway—next to him. He looked up, and I was amazed at his strange, rather colorful clothing. Then he said: "How nice to see each other here, Nora!"

He rolled his "r's" like an Italian. And to tell the truth, I really jumped when he said my name. I looked at him more closely, and since I've had a certain experience with historical figures encountering me, I considered who this person might be. And suddenly it occurred to me—he could only be . . .

"Excuse me, sir, I'm not quite sure who you are. But—might you be Petrarch?"

"Yes, quite right! But Nora, you needn't be so formal—I'm not unknown to you, after all, and I know you very well!"

"True. But tell me, where did you come from and how did you get here? You lived in Italy."

"But it is very interesting to compare the flowers and the natural world of both countries."

Yes, I can well understand Petrarch! We talked for quite a while, but then I had to go. You know, the Renaissance really is like spring! It breaks up winter's ice (metaphorically: the Middle Ages) and blooms naturally and freely and constantly "discovers" new things, for example, when new flowers and so on constantly sprout from the previously cold earth. In my history class, I have to give a little talk about the Renaissance in Italy. You can certainly tell me a lot about that.

Oh yes, I liked the comparison of the three skeptics to clowns. Clowns upset everything. Moreover, it contradicts the laws of nature, because it can do magic and cannot be defined. But clowns are figures of fun, and you really can't say that about these three men.

Now I have to close and run down to your place to give you the letter.

Yours, Nora

Essen, 16 February 1995

Dear Nora,

As you yourself saw by watching my eyes while I read your letter in your presence, what you wrote once again gave me great pleasure—my thanks to you and your whole family for such a lovely day at your place! This morning I immediately went to the café, which this time I had no difficulty in finding. It was pretty empty, but fortunately I met Socrates, who was sitting at the table next to me.

"Socrates," I said, "you remember Nora, don't you?"

"Nora? How can one forget her? Especially since Francesco is now driving us all crazy with her! Look at the table!"

And do you know what I saw? The first three letters of the name "Laura," which Francesco had carved on the table-top last spring, had been altered so that it now read "Nora."

"The things people do! Carving on tables—and then changing the names—that's disloyal."

"Don't be so severe, Vittorio," Socrates said. "It's almost spring, and Renaissance men are spring men. In addition, our friend has Italian blood. Moreover, he has good taste!"

"You're right again," I replied. "But since you are clearly one of her fans, tell me how to answer a question she asked me. The last time I met the infernal trio, with whom you are no doubt familiar. They confused me terribly and they confused Nora as well. However, what she found particularly striking was that at the end of my report of our encounter I mentioned that they seemed to me to have something important to say. But this is no more than an impression, and you must help me articulate it. You are an unconventional philosopher; sometimes you seem to be almost a skeptic, and at other times you very strongly criticize skeptics, at least in Plato's dialogues—though I'm not sure whether he represented you correctly."

"Let's put it this way: Plato represented and idealized certain traits of my personality and thought, and ignored others. Whether he represented the essential points, or whether, on the contrary, what he left out was still more central, depends on what my essence is—and that you have to discover for yourself. In any case, keep this in mind: Plato was by far my most brilliant student (a little too much of a blue-blood, perhaps, and his drive to arrive at certainty may have been too strong—but as a philosopher and as a writer he was a genius, and a truly great man into the bargain), and in representing a doctrine brilliance is an advantage as well as a danger. Anyhow, I'm very proud of him."

"I can easily understand that! But since he himself was certainly not a skeptic, I'd like the answer to Nora's question to come from you and not from him."

"Answer? I don't have any answers. I only ask questions."

"Okay, fine. Asking good questions is also very valuable, and if you want to use your questions and your art of midwifery to deliver a little spiritual child, I've no objection. So go ahead and ask!"

"Am I correct in assuming that you and Nora—the idealistic duo—still believe in truth?"

"You bet!"

"And you believe that what happens in the world has a meaning?"

"Naturally."

"Is skepticism a fundamental event in the world?"

"I believe one has to assent to that. From antiquity to the present, from Greece to Scotland there have always been skeptics."

"Thus skepticism must have a meaning—don't you think so?"

"Why?"

"Think about it for a minute. Didn't you just agree that whatever happens has a meaning?"

"Yes."

"Doesn't it follow that skepticism must also have a meaning?"

"Well . . . I'm afraid you're right."

"You don't need to be afraid. Whatever follows from true premises is true, and one must not fear the truth. So: if you two idealists are right, skepticism must have a secret meaning."

"What is it?"

"Are you asking me that—I who don't know anything? You have to discover it for yourself."

With that Socrates smiled so roguishly that I became somewhat annoyed.

"My dear Socrates, you must think I'm a dummy. I may be dumb insofar as there are many, many things I don't know but would really like to know. But I've noticed that *you claim* to be dumb, and yet know more than I do! I'm not so dumb that I wouldn't realize I was dealing with someone who's smarter than I am."

"So what is the goal of my (apparent) skepticism?"

"Well, you refuse to give me an answer; I'm supposed to figure it out for myself."

"And why should you figure it out for yourself?"

"Because we remember better what we've discovered by ourselves; we only make our own what we've worked out ourselves."

"What have you worked out with respect to a possible meaning of skepticism?"

"Skepticism, it seems, helps us to make ideas we've received from our education and from tradition our own, by questioning them—and then grounding them independently."

"Good, that's good to hear. But is skepticism important because of its questions alone, or is it also important because of its assertions?"

"I don't understand exactly what you mean."

"Do skeptics only ask questions? Don't they also make a number of assertions, for example that there is no truth, that there is no reason for things, that nothing follows rules?"

"They do, but those assertions are false."

"Do you know that, or only believe it?"

"I *know* it, because if a skeptic disputes the claim that there is truth, then he is contradicting himself; thus the opposite must be true!"

"So your knowledge—which is more than belief—is based on insight into the contradictory nature of the skeptical position?"

"You could probably say that."

"Thus without skeptics you couldn't *know* that there is truth?"

"Ah, Socrates, you've driven me into an embarrassing corner. It would be terrible to owe my knowledge to the skeptic. And yet I see that what I've already conceded forces me to accept this consequence."

"Maybe now you understand why I am partly skeptic, and partly a critic of skeptics. Passing through skepticism put me through a trial by fire, so to speak; only after I was a skeptic did I move from being a believer to a knower."

"Oh, Socrates, I'll have to think about that for a long time and talk with Nora."

"Nora may not understand it all yet," said a familiar voice from the back of the café. I turned around and recognized Giambattista. "As a guardian philosopher with an interest in laws of development I must first state my own position. Nora is not yet capable of adequately grasping the meaning of skepticism. She is a child, and therefore still in the phase of belief. Not until puberty, into which she will probably soon enter, will our little Nora develop strong doubts about all her previous views. Like all young people, she will go through a crisis. But I have three reasons for hoping that this crisis will not overcome her—that on the contrary, she will pass it with flying colors. First, she has already understood why we have to pass through doubt in order to acquire a deeper grip on truth. Second, she is lucky that most of her beliefs are true. She will not have to distance herself so much from her family as other people who don't come from such an open-minded home; she has only to learn how to give her beliefs a deeper foundation. Third, I am here—as her guardian philosopher, I will watch over her development. In all the confusion that the infernal trio may yet inflict on her, she should hang on to a basic trust in this world."

Now, isn't that something, Nora? Through all the difficulties that life may bring (and that make it interesting, moreover), don't forget this: the world is beautiful, and you must contribute to its beauty through what you are and will still become.

Warmest greetings, Vittorio

---

16 March 1995

Dear Vittorio,

I've finally gotten around to writing you. But tomorrow I won't be going to school, because I have a cough and sniffles. Thanks for the wonderful letter, which helped clear up my confusion! I was very glad to get it and read it over and over (as always). Now, however, I must tell you right away what just happened to me! A few days ago I was sitting at my desk reading your letter—not suspecting anything; the door that goes from my room out to the balcony stood open. I was thinking about skepticism, when someone tapped me on the shoulder and said: "Ah! You're reading Vittorio's letter! Can you now more or less make out his handwriting?"

Frightened, I turned around and saw Giambattista standing behind me!

"Giambattista! How nice of you to have come here! Yes, if my parents read the letter out loud a couple of times then I can manage; and if I can't read some of the words, I can at least get the gist!"

"If I am now your guardian philosopher, I have to visit you sometimes. Moreover, today is a special occasion: there's going to be a little party in the courtyard of the café, and I'd like it very much if you could come too. What do you say?"

"That would be great."

"Good! Then put on something that will make it harder to recognize you! Otherwise we'll have half the guests on our hands. And dress warmly, so you don't get cold. We're going to fly."

I understood, and quickly put on a warm jacket and a headscarf; then Giambattista took me by the hand and we flew over the housetops to the café, or rather, to the courtyard of the café. On the way,

Giambattista asked me, "Now, Nora, what do you think about skepticism?"

"I see its theoretical importance. I understand what you and Socrates mean, and also what Vittorio means. But I have a really hard time imagining that I will give up my present beliefs. Maybe my opinions will change, but it's so difficult to think that I will stop being intuitive, and no longer love fairy tales and legends, and so on, as we children do."

"Yes, I understand. But Nora, it is definitely not good to give up many beliefs. On the contrary, one should try to maintain childlike abilities. It's only with their help that one can develop and grow up. You know, this development occurs not only among individuals but also among peoples. Think of ancient Greece. At first people were in the "childish stage." The Greeks believed in gods, created myths, etc., and then they entered into the age of heroes, when the rich became dominant, and slaves and poor people were oppressed. Women too, unfortunately! But then these lower classes became restless; slaves and other people began to doubt whether everything they were told was true. That was the period of skepticism. Finally came the age of philosophy, literature, etc.—and there we see maturity."

I nodded. Then I asked him: "Giambattista, what stage do you think I'm in right now?"

"I'm not sure, but you might be in the age of heroes!"

We remained silent for a while. Then I said: "I can hardly wait for the time when I might become skeptical! —Tell me, Giambattista, does this kind of development take place all over the world?"

He didn't seem to be listening any more, however, because he cried: "Look, some of them have already gathered down there on the other side of the river [see letter no. 1]. You can already almost see the whole café, and there's the courtyard!"

Slowly we floated down into the courtyard. (No one was surprised that we flew in by air.) Giambattista said it would be safer if we sat at one of the tables set up at the back of the courtyard, because then there would be less danger that someone would recognize me. He ordered us two cups of hot chocolate—on that day probably no one was drinking water, because it was a celebration. Gradually all the guests came in, and almost all of them were involved in lively discussion. (Many of them were also arguing.) However, I saw not only philosophers but also other, younger people. We were in the courtyard of the café, after all. But then it was announced that—here I could hardly believe my ears—*Einstein* (!) wanted to play the violin. First a couple of Mozart sonatas and then a well-known children's song. And it was true—Einstein appeared in casual clothing, with a jovial look on his face, and white, unruly hair. He played beautifully, and at the end, when he was playing the children's song, I saw that his ears were wiggling in time with the music. He was wiggling his ears! Then lots of other people sat down beside him and began to wiggle their ears, too. I would have liked to join them, but Giambattista said again that it would be too risky.

"Too dumb," I thought. Apparently Einstein had seen the somewhat bad-tempered look on my face. In any case, when he had finished, he came toward our table. We both praised his violin-playing, but then he suddenly looked at me more closely and then cried, "Nora! . . ."

He didn't get any further, because Giambattista put his hand over his mouth. "We don't want a mad rush," he explained.

After the two of them had talked for a while, Giambattista asked me: "Nora, what are you reading right now? As your guardian philosopher I have a right to know that!"

"I'm reading Jostein Gaarder's 'The Christmas Mystery,' 'Quo Vadis,' and Plato's 'Phaedo.'"

"Fine, fine. So you're reading the 'Phaedo'! Socrates's death, yes, yes . . ."

"Yes, I think it's really good the way Socrates so confidently drank the cup of hemlock. How lucky he was to have become an idealist before he died! Otherwise he probably wouldn't have believed in his immortal soul! People who believe that their soul disappears along with their bodies and that people will soon forget them must be very sad," I said.

Albert agreed with me: "Yes, that's right! I, too, was not afraid of death. And as you see, I had no reason to fear it, for I can go on living very well here. Only as a soul, of course, but that doesn't matter."

I asked, "Do you think Socrates was not afraid because he intuitively knew that there must be something good after death, or because he had arrived at that view by reasoning?"

"Both, I think!" Giambattista said.

What do you think, Vittorio? Then I said: "I also know a fairy tale by Hans Christian Andersen that deals with death and the immortal soul. It's called 'The Little Mermaid.' I like it very much."

We went on talking about this and that, and then I had to go home. Giambattista flew me back to my room. I thought it was too bad that you weren't also at the party, but probably you had too much to do because of your trip to Korea?—

You know, my geography teacher thinks human beings are descended from apes! I know lots of other people who think that, too. Do you also believe it? I'm not at all sure, since although the first human beings resembled apes in certain ways, they also had understanding and a soul, didn't they? And this soul cannot have developed so simply as that! Do you think souls develop?

Right now I'm looking out the window, and it's raining very hard. The raindrops are just driving through the air! Bells are also ringing. There's something festive in the air and in everything! A strange seagull is flying by up in the sky . . . Sometimes I think that they are heralds of a great, great celebration . . . I'm not sure myself what I mean by that.—

Now I have to run to the mailbox, so my letter will arrive tomorrow! For you that's probably "today!" We all wish you a wonderful trip to Korea! Will you tell me all about it when you get back?

Warmest greetings from everybody,
Nora

———

Seoul, 27 March 1995

Dear Nora,

It was a real joy to find your letter waiting for me when I came back from Paris late in the evening in order to leave for Korea the next day. It confirms what the organizers of the first UNESCO meeting on philosophy apparently thought: philosophy is too serious a subject to leave to adults alone! At the meeting in Paris, where many important philosophers spoke, there were also a few schoolchildren who had a chance to ask the famous philosopher Michel Serres some questions. The most important one, which was asked by an eight-year-old girl, was "Why is the world the way it is, and not otherwise?" Serres answered: "The world could also be otherwise, and from the bottom of my heart I hope that by the end of your life it will be different because of what you will have done!"

How would you have answered this question? And what question would you have asked? (Asking questions is almost as important as answering them.)

So, now I've been in the Far East for a good week. It has been a rather strenuous but also fascinating experience I wouldn't want to have missed. This is the first time I've been in a non-European country that has successfully coped with the modernization process—and has managed in just a few decades to establish a reasonable and fairly well-distributed prosperity. This is all the more amazing because, first, other non-European cultures (outside East Asia) have not been able to do the same, at least not as well; and second, because these other cultures are more closely related to European culture than are East Asian cultures. The Islamic world believes in a single God and was influenced by Greek culture, and we are related even linguistically with the Indians. In contrast, Europe is connected only marginally with East Asia—and yet this cultural milieu will soon become the center of worldwide development and become the successor of European industry. On one hand, I'm very happy about this country's achievement—here one is spared the encounter with the terrible poverty one sees in India. On the other hand, one feels a certain uneasiness: if the whole world became a big Europe or North America, then the fundamental ecosystems would break down, and independently of these consequences, the modernization process inflicts deplorable damage on the human soul.

Nora, when you are an adult, you will be able to preserve the childlike vitality of your soul, but will all people and all cultures be able to do so as well? I doubt it very much, and it would be terrible if the world finally came to the point at which every spark of the divine—that is, the childlike—age died out. Perhaps that's why cultures develop with differing degrees of rapidity and effectiveness? So that reserves are maintained that dry up in most people when they reach the age of reason? I was quite saddened when yesterday Hu Nam and I visited an old Korean village that had been reconstructed, and she told me that in her childhood this world still existed, whereas today residents of Seoul have to travel an hour outside their capital to see silkworms or even dogs and chickens. A whole world that had lasted for centuries has disappeared in thirty years—isn't that a thought that makes a chill run down your spine? If, like Socrates, you're convinced of the immortality of the soul, the death of an individual is moving, but the death of an entire form of life is even more moving. What do you think?

However, Korea has not simply become a modern country with high-rise buildings, cars, and computers. What your guardian philosopher once wrote, namely that rivers carry their fresh water far out into the sea, and similarly, that cultures preserve their earlier stages, applies to Korea as well. Female shamans still play an important role in Korean society (a few days ago, Hu Nam and I visited a famous fortune-teller); in modern buildings the fourth story is indicated by a letter that suggests good luck and not by the number, because in East Asia the number 4 stands for death, and people are afraid of it. The relationships between people are much more formal than in Europe; people bow reverently to professors. Even from the language you can tell how people respond to an interlocutor and how much importance they attach to his social position. To a question like "Is he at home?" they reply "*Yes,* he is not at home," or "*No,* he is at home," putting the emphasis not on the fact inquired about but on the interlocutor's question. So-called honorifics, categories of the verbal system that don't exist in our language, are also interesting. Germans distinguish between "Du" and "Sie," of course, but a sentence such as "the table is small" is formulated in the same way by all those involved in a conversation. In Korean, in contrast, the verb has a different form depending on whom one is speaking to. What do you think about the relationship between language and thought? Does thought influence language, or does language shape thought?

On the flight to Seoul we crossed China. As we flew over Peking, it was so cloudy we couldn't see anything, but I got a good view of Shanghai: a huge city spreads out from a big river, and one positively feels the hectic activities of the people down below. China is also becoming a prosperous modern state, I think.

As I was thinking about why East Asia is so good at modernizing itself, I suddenly couldn't believe my eyes: looking out the window of the plane, I saw an old Chinese man sitting on the wing! "I hope to God he doesn't fall off," I thought. Upset, I turned toward my seatmate, who seemed not to see anything unusual, even though he was looking in the same direction. I looked at the wing again, and the old man waved to me. I finally understood: aha, a philosopher! While Nora can fly through the air with Giambattista, unfortunately I have to take a real airplane and make my contribution to polluting the environment. But after their deaths, true philosophers can fly like children again, and they sit on the wings of metal birds only when they want to have a conversation with airplane passengers.

In the meantime, the Chinese man had pointed to himself, and then all of a sudden I understood what he wanted to say. It was Confucius, and he was answering my question: Confucianism is the basis of the East Asian economic miracle.

"Do you like this development?" I asked him.

"Well, so long as the family remains intact, I've got nothing against it—on the contrary, because it increases the fame of the Middle Kingdom."

"But I have a great deal against it," said another Chinese whom I had not previously noticed; he had been sitting right behind Confucius, but he now moved into my field of vision. "The well already didn't seem that huge to me—what should I say about today's world? Haven't you noticed that with all these machines people's hearts are steadily becoming more machinelike? Where is the Tao in all this?"

"Should we then renounce all technology, Chuang-tzu? And if not, where precisely is the boundary beyond which we must not go?"

"That is a difficult question, Vittorio, and I can give you only an approximate answer. But if you no longer feel the beauty of mountains and water, if you can no longer rejoice like a child, then you have gone too far. So enjoy the beauty of the landscape, and think of Nora and think like Nora; then perhaps it will be defensible that you have taken this airplane."

I also wanted to ask him what he thought about the descent of human beings from apes (I presume that since it is a sign of human beings' bond with nature he would not disapprove of it), but we were already preparing to land, and Chuang-tzu and Confucius, taking each other by the hand, had already jumped off the airplane's wing and were now fluttering through the air, going eastward toward Japan.

Dear Nora, I hope you all, and especially your dear grandmother, are well, and I greet you most heartily as

Your Vittorio

---

27 May 1995

Dear Vittorio,

Do you know where I'm sitting right now? In the sand, between two dunes. I can see the sea through the beach grass and hear its roar. The tide is going out. The sky is gray, but there's still a little blue over the sea. A few people are going up and down the beach, and one of them has his dog with him. At the horizon, the sea and the sky merge. It's very beautiful here on Juist. It's a little island standing out in the sea. The sea often seems infinite, because you can't see any end to it. But there are practically no trees here, and I miss them a little. A light rain has begun to fall—I'll probably have to continue this letter inside. Are you feeling better? I hope so—get well soon!

Monday we will be home again, and then you can come visit us for a few days. Maybe then it won't be so boring for you, because you're not allowed to read on account of your eyes. I'd read to you. But then you'll have to bring the translation of Leibniz, because I can't yet read French. Anyway, Vittorio, you were pretty careless when you read so many little letters and when you were constantly looking at your previous computer, which had such small print. One mustn't treat one's body so carelessly, because God has given it to us and awakened it into life, and it is unique besides!

Please excuse me for taking such a long time to write you. I've really had a lot to do lately and there's more work coming up. But I would still like to go on writing. Vittorio, when you write to me, couldn't you print the letter with the computer? Or maybe write more clearly, please. It's always very hard for me to decipher your writing, and I can never read your letter without help.

Now about Korea: Yes, I agree, it's sad when a culture dies. But I'm not sure that the death of a culture can be compared with the death of a person. Culture is, after all, produced by people. Moreover, I don't believe that Korea's progress from the old culture to technology was absolutely bad and that it could be said that it would be better to return to earlier times. Earlier cultures weren't perfect, either. You can't say that the present time is a deviation, because then all other periods would have to be deviations too, since none of them were really desirable. I believe one ought to say instead that we should begin over anew, act differently, and see what we could make better, don't you think? We idealists say that everything has a meaning. And Vittorio, the culture is still spiritually available! It has given us something, and we have developed it.

I've also thought that maybe all three of the great periods of development throughout the world are necessary. The age of the gods, the age of doubt, and the age of maturity. Although it occurs to me just now to wonder which country is really in the age of maturity! Maturity would really have to be a synthesis—that is, it would have to be good . . . Maybe we are waiting for this synthesis—or we have to achieve it ourselves.

You also asked whether I thought language influenced thought or thought influenced language. I believe that in Korea thought influenced language. I can't think of any country where that isn't so. Do you know of one? Your meeting with the two philosophers on the airplane wing was very exciting. I tend to side with Chuang-tzu.

I don't understand why Confucius thinks the family is so much more important than the problem of technology and environmental pollution. In fact, why is the family so important at all? Can you explain that to me? Anyway. You talked about the limits of technology. Chuang-tzu said that the boundary is at the point where you notice that you've lost your sense of the beauty of nature. I believe that may not be quite enough, because then you could fly in airplanes everyday if you still found forests beautiful. Nature also has to be important to you, because you don't do that on your own. In two weeks, Mama has to write a report explaining why people should protect the environment, why that is necessary, and what must move people to do it. I find this subject very important and interesting, because it determines our future in certain ways. One of my classmates and I want to form a club to which we would admit a few members who still haven't noticed how beautiful life is and how precious it is, and we want to show them that. We say it would be an environmental club; in particular, we want to work on behalf of the rainforest and its inhabitants. But we also want to protest against nouveau-riche consumers.

This time I haven't met a regular philosopher, but only a "half-philosopher." As I was sitting on Juist, I suddenly noticed an old man sitting down next to me. He had a white beard and bushy eyebrows, under which there were what at first seemed to be rather fierce eyes. He smiled at me. Then I understood that it was Theodor Storm. I am currently reading one of his novellas, and I have also seen a few pictures of him. But you don't really need pictures if you want to recognize someone. In any case, I recognized him, and with his index finger he pointed to a vague figure on the dike. He smiled at me expectantly. I squinted in order to see him better, because his form was very shadowy and, as I said, vague. I shrugged my shoulders. I tried to show him that I couldn't recognize the figure. Then he tapped my forehead with his finger and said: "Close your eyes, Nora, and you'll be able to see him clearly."

I thought he'd gone crazy. Since when do you have to close your eyes in order to see better? But then I had an idea. I closed my eyes and tried to see with the inner eye. And then I recognized the Rider on the White Horse riding along the dike. I opened my eyes, and now I could see him that way too. His cape fluttered behind him—his white horse's hoofs thundered on the solid dike. I smiled at Theodor—I had understood. I think the Rider on the White Horse is appropriate to our subject, don't you? However, then I had to leave. I had to go back for dinner, and moreover I'd promised Bettina to watch the sunset with her.—

Finally, it occurred to me that the soul, as "eternal spirit," doesn't actually live, but rather "is." What is living passes away. And after death the soul no longer has an earthly memory like ours? It has no knowledge, it simply "is." But it makes matter live. Matter and soul together produce life. Thus all life has a soul, and none of it is without worth, as the Nazis for example tried to say.

In addition, I've not yet thanked you for the flower seeds you sent me a few weeks ago by way of Mama. Thanks very much for them. The flowers are not yet in bloom, but they are already about ten centimeters tall. I'm looking forward to seeing them bloom.

You asked me, in connection with your meeting where a French school class was able to ask a philosopher questions, how I would have answered the question "Why is the world the way it is and not otherwise?" and what kind of question I would have asked.

It's really hard to say anything about the first question. The French philosopher answered it so well, and I can hardly add anything.

Maybe one could say that it is the way it is simply because God created it that way. Or that because we human beings are the culmination of creation, we actually are responsible for the world—and maybe the world is the way it is because we don't correctly perceive this responsibility. Human beings have to use their great power responsibly. Moreover—if human beings are the culmination of creation, they are a great danger to God. However, I think things will become better someday—for sure!

You know, Vittorio, there are so many, many questions we can ask, and for which I'd so much like to have answers. Maybe you can help me answer two of them:

1. Is the universe infinite?
2. Does time have an end, and will Paradise come someday?

Dear Vittorio, I hope you get better soon! Do come to our house next weekend. One of my girlfriends is also coming this weekend. Then you could meet her, and we could ask you lots of questions and talk with you, if you aren't too tired and feel like it! Mama, Papa, Grandma, and Bettina would also be very happy if you could come. We'd also put the ointment in your eyes. It would be so great! You could sleep a lot and rest up. And I'd also read to you!

Now it's gradually getting dark. Swifts are flying through the air and everything is getting green! Including the flowers whose seed you sent me!

See you soon,
Nora

---

5 June 1995

Dear Nora,

Your letter and your cassette, which I've listened to many times, were a great pleasure for me; I believe they helped my eyes get better.

I found particularly sensitive your observation that we really see some things only when we shut our eyes—a great consolation for someone in my condition.

The last few weeks have given me an opportunity to think over many things that I have done in my life, for good or not so good, and you are surely right that one of the not so good things is that I have not sufficiently husbanded my strengths. Still, I spent this weekend in your hospitable home, and was able to relax.

Your dear Mama is even so kind as to write this letter for me—sparing not only my eyes but also yours! You won't have any difficulty reading your mother's beautiful handwriting. It was a great pleasure to meet your best friend yesterday. At your age there is hardly anything more important than finding friends of your own age with whom you can battle your way through the age of heroes.

In this phase it is moreover comprehensible that you would have difficulty with Confucius's view regarding the enormous importance of the family—because you have to take the first steps outside the family. But precisely you, who have had such exceptional good luck with your whole family, should not too greatly doubt that the family is the basic institution: in it the young person first experiences the community that has to support the individual.

In your letter, there is much that is noteworthy; it pleased me very much that you ultimately consider the individual more important than a culture, because a culture consists only of individuals. No less important is your insight that an idealist should not complain about comprehensive developments, but rather discover their meaning. In actuality, even if the process of modernization is problematic in many regards—in it a power prevails that is more than human, yet we have to go through it anyway. Hegel once described the Greek world this way: if nostalgia were allowed, we would feel it for that land, for that condition; but he uses the contrary-to-fact subjunctive "were" because he thinks that one has to come to terms with the time in which one lives, without yearning for other times.

We can't go backward, but we want to work to make the future better—just as you are doing with your club. Your reflections about the soul are very interesting, even if I didn't entirely understand them. If I interpret you correctly, your view is that only something that can die, and is therefore material, can be said to be alive: a flower is alive, an animal is alive—in general, organisms are alive. But one cannot say that God is alive, and one cannot say that a bodiless soul is alive, either. Is that what you meant to say?

You try to answer the question why the world is as it is by saying that God just created it that way. However, that leads to the further question, why God created the world that way and not another. Was His choice completely free? Or did He proceed in accord with certain criteria? Finally, you attribute to humans a special responsibility for the current condition of the world, for example when you write that humans are a great danger to God, precisely because they are the culmination of creation. But then hasn't God foreseen—or perhaps even predetermined—what humans would do, so that their actions could ultimately be attributed to God? That is at least one of the controversial questions we have discussed many times, but which is now once again urgent.

Dear Nora, neither of your questions is easy to answer, and for now I'll have to limit myself to commenting on the first one: is the world spatially finite or infinite? I thought about this question for a long time, and encountered the usual objections: if the world were finite, then you could go to the boundary and stick your arm over it—but then there would be something on the other side of the boundary. But an infinite world is also disturbing—it seems to lack measure and order. As I walked around in your beautiful garden, mulling over this problem, I suddenly saw two men who were loudly arguing with one another. The first was about thirty years older than the second, and apart from their violent confrontation you could discern certain similarities between them.

"Calm down, gentlemen," I said, interrupting their argument. "Don't fight; instead, tell me what it's all about, and then tell me who you are."

The older man bowed politely and introduced himself: "Bolyai, mathematician."

The young man also bowed, and said: "Bolyai, mathematician."

I was bewildered; was I witnessing a personality split? Both of them seemed to read my mind, for they answered in chorus: "No, your honor, you are witnessing something much worse—a split in truth."

I was astounded, and the older man said: "My whole life had a single goal—to prove the truth of Euclidean geometry. I gladly concede that I did not get as far as I had hoped—but what my son has derived from my work clearly goes too far."

"Well, I have simply shown that the propositions of Euclidean geometry are not necessarily true—*if* we posit the axiom regarding parallel lines, *then* it is valid. But we can also posit a different axiom, and then a different geometry is valid."

"That's dreadful!" his father cried. "Geometry is not something that can depend on arbitrary assumptions. The whole value of truth goes down the drain if there are several, mutually incompatible truths."

I too was at a loss, since in fact it seemed to me that a great deal depended on the outcome of this confrontation between father and son. "Gentlemen, perhaps you could answer the question that concerns my friend Nora—is space finite or infinite?"

"Euclid's unique space is obviously infinite," the old man replied. "Every limited plane can be extended—every limit is arbitrary."

"The issue has to be seen in a more differentiated way," the younger man said. "One can imagine systems of axioms according to which space is necessarily finite. Imagine the surface of a sphere. According to the usual conception, it is the limit of a three-dimensional figure, namely a sphere. But one can imagine that it is the true two-dimensional shape, the true original plane. On it one can in fact always move further without ever encountering a limit, but it is nonetheless a finite surface."

"But that would be only a two-dimensional shape; do you think that space is two-dimensional, then?"

"Of course not—one has only to imagine three-dimensional space as analogous to the surface of a sphere. Then it would be finite, but not limited."

"But no one can imagine such a space," his father cried. "That is completely out of the question, because such a curved, three-dimensional space could only be conceived within a four-dimensional Euclidean space, and it is absolutely impossible to visualize shapes that are more than three-dimensional."

"That is true," the son conceded, "but it is an error to believe that the limits of our ability to visualize coincide with the limits of our cognitive capacities. We can calculate with such geometries, and that suffices."

After these words, the two men disappeared. The conversation really upset me. On one hand, I understand the father's fear that the beauty of geometry would be endangered if there were more than one geometry. On the other hand, it would be fascinating if we could solve your problem in such an elegant way by means of a non-Euclidean geometry. Are you comfortable with the younger Bolyai's suggestion, or do you think that it is dangerous to leave the boundaries of our view of space behind us? Given the poor state of my eyes, I must admit that the idea that thinking is not dependent on visualization appeals to me . . .

> *Warmest greetings from your friend with bad eyes*
> *but a good spiritual view of your being,*
> *Vittorio*

---

10 July 1995

Dear Vittorio,

Many thanks for your letter. I was very glad to get it, but what the younger Bolyai said was pretty hard to understand. You know, at first I didn't understand it at all, and thought about it for a long time, but now it has already become clearer to me what Bolyai meant. And it's really exciting to think that many basic assumptions could be replaced by others. But it's also dangerous, because that way you let much of the "framework" of humanity simply "collapse." Moreover, there would be more than one truth. I believe that there is an objective truth. Otherwise God would not exist, either! Maybe we human beings can't find out everything, and maybe that's good. But all the same we can think something that we can no longer imagine, for example, that a sphere is two-dimensional. Or God. However, I believe that there is a little spark of objective truth in everyone. One of Bolyai's ideas I also found interesting was that in the universe as a whole opposites are transcended: space is finite, but has no boundaries. So I asked myself whether in God opposites are also transcended. We already discussed that question once, but then it occurred to me again. And now the question whether God was free when He created the world. If in God opposites are more or less transcended, then the opposition between good and evil is also transcended, and God would also have evil within Him. And then evil would come into the world through God Himself.

On the other hand, evil could also come from an evil opposing power, such as the devil, perhaps.

Or evil could result from human freedom. Then God would have taken a chance in creating human beings, but what if he could foresee that?

I'm mostly concerned with the first and third theses. If God is a synthesis of everything that is actually the highest of all, then there would also be evil in God.

But somehow that's a really weird idea, don't you think? It makes the thought of God so objective, so lifeless. If God took a risk when He created human beings, because He gave us freedom, then the world might have a clearer meaning. Then our task would be to drive evil out of the world or at least to destroy the evil within ourselves. I think that is a splendid, if difficult, task. But we come back to the thesis that God took a risk. This is the idea I really like best. However, it might make God a little too human. The other conception is more logical. (Can you "work" on this subject with logic?)

And if God could create only good, then he would not be the highest! Then there would still have to be an antithesis and a thesis! Oh—this is so hard, so unimaginable! Maybe we all have a personal idea of God that is true for us, because we can't grasp objective truth.

But are we humans so lacking in knowledge on this point?—

Yes, you correctly understood what I wrote about the soul. I think that after death it passes over into another state. It can "live" only in connection with the body. And life passes away. Thus God can't really "live" either, otherwise He would not be eternal. What do you think about that, Vittorio? You wrote out a sentence from Hegel for me that is very beautiful. But I don't entirely understand why we must not yearn for things. Because it's only by yearning for something better that we are driven to realize our wishes and yearnings in actuality. However, I think Hegel said that in another context, didn't he?

You know, Vittorio, recently I've wished I could fly like a bird! Then I could dance through sky, glide along and soar up to higher realms! That would be really wonderful.

The bells of the old city church have just struck seven o'clock. It's already dark—and there's thunder and lightning and light rain. It's pleasantly cool but not cold. The darkness is calming. Whenever I look at the sky for a long time, many thoughts go through my head.

Today we got our report cards, and after the church service we said goodbye to our teacher. (She is getting a new class, and we get a new teacher.) Tomorrow we're going to England. I'm already looking forward to it. Who knows whom I might meet there! In Cornwall there are lots of cliffs and caves. King Arthur and the knights of the Round Table must have lived around there somewhere. Exciting, huh?

I'll write to you from England!

And then when we get back, you must come visit us again (or we'll visit you).

Your recent visit was great!

See you soon,
Nora

[Written on the envelope:]
P.S. Tomato vines grew from the flower seeds you sent us! Two tomatoes are already hanging on them, but they're still green!

Essen, 14 July 1995

Dear Nora,

Once again, it was a great pleasure to get your letter this morning; I'd been waiting for it so long! Many thanks! Forgive me for writing my reply by hand, but this way I can write to you outside in the open air, and also I find computer print very impersonal. As you know, our correspondence is very important to me; I write letters to boring colleagues on computers, but not to the girl par excellence! Maybe the magician Merlin will help you decipher my handwriting? You'll surely run into him in Cornwall, and since he's an old childhood friend of mine, he'll find it easy to assist you. Or else you can call upon our common friend Sherlock Holmes, who has already solved more difficult problems than deciphering my inkblots. I hear he has come to the conclusion that the basic questions of rational theology are even more stimulating than tracking down Moriarty, especially since God's complexity really consists in His being inconceivable, and this exceeds our confused understanding—especially that of the petty schemers who are caught in the labyrinth of their own lies. Only if we ourselves can become simple can we understand God, even if our understanding always remains approximate.

In this conviction I came into the café, still mulling over your questions. As a result of a lucky accident—or divine Providence—four gentlemen were sitting at a table, discussing "the problem of evil," apparently oblivious of the heat. One of them looked as if he came from the Near East, and had clearly had an eventful life; he spoke energetically and passionately.

"Evil can never, ever come from God," he cried, "God is good; evil has nothing to do with Him. Therefore it must proceed from a principle of evil, from an opposing god—Ahriman, the enemy of Ahura Mazda. There are two original powers."

"But my dear Zarathustra," replied a gentle man with very large eyes, "Only one can be God. If there are two principles, both of them are still principles, and they have something in common—the fact that they are principles. The absolute is precisely that: we cannot get around the fact that the pinnacle of being is the One."

"My dear Plotinus, is the One the Good then?"

"Certainly; whatever unites and connects is good. Conflict is bad. Duality is incompatible with the divine."

"Then where does evil come from?"

"Evil is merely a lack of good. It *is* nothing true. It only arises near nothingness, far away from the fullness of being. We would do better to keep silent about it, because there is nothing in it to discover."

"You're wrong," Zarathustra said heatedly. "Evil *is!* And how! Illness may be the dissolution of an organism, but evil things are powerful, produce effects, destroy—perhaps in the end they destroy even themselves, but before they do they destroy many other things. Lofty indifference to evil is false—we have to battle against evil, take it seriously, get involved with it . . ."

"Even at the risk of becoming similar to it?" Plotinus broke in melancholically. I had been following the exchange so intently that I had not yet really noticed the two other philosophers. One of them had a very reflective, blotchy face—it was Hans Jonas! He winked at me and asked if the Hans Jonas Society had been included on the register of associations yet, and then entered the discussion.

"Plotinus, there's nothing you can do about the existence of evil—unfortunately! I wish you were right—but this century at least has given your thesis the lie. There has always been evil, but the power put in its hands by the modern state has given it a reality it could only dream of earlier . . ."

"I had understood your criticism of our friend Immanuel as claiming that being and the good were also closely connected," Plotinus politely interrupted. "But never mind. Where did you get the idea of evil, if it exists? From God?"

"Absolutely not! God expressed Himself in the creation of the world—as the voice of the moral law, warning and demanding, He hovers over the world; but the world is determined by its own laws, which include chance as well, and in human beings this chance takes the form of freedom, freedom to choose good as well as evil."

"Really?" asked the fourth gentleman at the table in a calm and relaxed voice. He was wearing an enormous wig, and when he saw that I did not recognize him, he bowed to me with exquisite courtesy, and briefly introduced himself: "Gottfried of Hanover." (Whom does that make you think of? But it was not our mutual friend; I had already recognized him.) Then he turned toward Hans Jonas again.

"There are two things that still trouble me a little about your conception, and I beg you to explain how you would resolve my problems. First, your God seems to me rather too weak. He is certainly not omnipotent, and presumably not omniscient either, for then He probably would have not expressed Himself in this way, foreseeing what would come of this limitation on His power in the world. If God is omniscient and omnipotent, then he cannot have willed the existence of evil (for it would be sacrilegious to think that), but He could have tolerated it. And why? Because from the overcoming of evil more good would come than from a world without evil. —The second difficulty that I have with your interesting assertion is the following: you seem to assume that human beings can act without any ground. But we must always inquire into the ground of an assertion and into the cause of an event. Anyone who knows someone well can often say quite precisely how he came to his decision. And the more moral a person is, the more sure one can be that he will do what is good. If freedom were something positive, then it would be a lack, and the unforeseeable would be valuable. But tell me, Hans, could you commit an evil act?"

"Your second question puts me in an embarrassing position, my dear Gottfried. As to your first, I would say this: not all attributes that tradition ascribes to God are necessarily attributable to Him in reality. I much prefer a God who is not omnipotent to a God who does evil."

"Does? Not at all! He merely does not prevent it, because good will develop out of it . . ."

At that moment a man with a powerful body and meditative eyes came up to the table, a cobbler's awl in his hand.

"Forgive me if I am butting into your discussion, but it's simply too important! Gottfried, your distinction between commission and omission is not persuasive when we are talking about God. If *I* fail to help someone, that is not so bad as when I harm someone, because for me the concrete act of helping is a far greater effort than its omission. If it costs me nothing to help someone, and I fail to do so, then I am just as guilty as if I harmed someone—unless in the interest of the other person's autonomy intervention is not permissible. But according to you, God is omnipotent, and what He creates is the self, not an intervention in the self; thus it becomes pointless to distinguish between commission and omission."

"What are you trying to say?"

"That evil has to be in God in some way, but of course only as a component of His nature, which makes itself independent in the world. God is not pure positivity; the negative must also be included within Him."

"Bravo, Jakob!" cried a sixth thinker, who suddenly stood up. It was Hegel, and he clapped the previous speaker on the back. "The Absolute must be a synthesis of the positive and the negative—not merely a union, but rather a union of unity and multiplicity. *Nemo contra Deum nisi Deus ipse!*"

At this point I dared to intervene in the discussion among these great philosophers. "Dear Hegel, my friend Nora would like you to say why yearning is not allowed."

"Because, as Gottfried rightly maintains, we live in the best of all possible worlds—longing is dissatisfaction with the present, and hence ungratefulness to God."

"But there is much that is negative in the best of all possible worlds; maybe some periods, although necessary, are less happy than others. In those periods, isn't one allowed to yearn for something better?"

"No, because the present is always better than the past."

"Hegel, if I may say so, there you are mistaken," cried Jonas passionately. "History is full of the most dreadful lapses in moral con-

sciousness. Your optimism is irresponsible, and anyway, the idea of responsibility presupposes freedom."

The discussion grew more heated; and since I knew that Jonas
didn't like Hegel, I decided to leave—Plotinus at least will understand why I avoided quarrels. In any case, it seemed to me that these
dead souls were still very passionate . . . But at the door I was briefly
held up by a man whom I had never seen before.

"These thinkers are going to argue for a long time. They are all pro-
ceeding on a false premise—that these questions can be resolved by
reason; it is incapable of resolving them. We have to simply believe in
what our own hearts tell us."

"Well, I'm glad my friend Nora has both a good heart and good reasoning power," I replied. "Thus there seems to be no absolute contradiction between them."

And I escaped from him in order to write you this letter.

Dear Nora, I sincerely hope you are all enjoying your vacation in
England, and send you my heartiest greetings.

Yours, Vittorio

---

1 August 1995

Dear Vittorio,

Thanks for your letter. Unfortunately, this card is not my full reply,
but only a preview. Just now we are in the busy city of Cambridge, far
from the sea and from Merlin and Arthur. I like the city with all its
colleges and churches . . . But it reminds me of Italy. On the farm in
Devon/Cornwall it was very beautiful. There you could pursue your
thoughts and think up stories. You can see a long way over the rather
hilly country. The cliffs on the coast and at Land's End were beautiful, but also very melancholy. I like England. Here you see extremely
different, interesting things from almost all historical periods!

Until the next letter,
Nora

---

15 August 1995

Dear Vittorio,

How pleased I was, about three weeks ago, to be holding your letter
in my hands in England, on a very beautiful, comfortable, authentic

English farm. Little Ben, the farmer's son, brought it to me. So—thanks a lot!

Did you get my card? Then you certainly know that I grew fond of England. The whole feeling of life there is different from what it is here in Germany. The people are also different: they are much more open, friendlier, and also more willing to help. Once I went to school with the daughter, Phillippa, who is also twelve, and attended classes all day long. During the recesses a great many pupils crowded around me like a bunch of grapes and asked who I was and where I came from, offered to be my friends and helped me when they could. I think that in Germany we would hesitate to approach a foreigner so freely. Maybe not only because of a lack of interest, but more because we are brought up to maintain a certain distance. And England itself as a country also pleased me very much. Everywhere you can see traces of the past, from almost every period. From the Celts to the counties and the cloisters, from the Middle Ages to early modern times.

However, in many places the landscape is somewhat melancholic. Once we drove to "Land's End." There were the thundering waves and raw cliffs at the end of England. Behind us the moor grasses and flowers were blowing in the wind, and before us was the great sea and the cliffs. It's a place that puts you in more of a reflective than a cheery mood. Anyway, there I had to think about our powers of imagination and our reason. The sea might be an example of them: we can see the water only as far as the horizon. Then we see nothing more, but we know that it continues on beyond the horizon.

But we also went to cities like Tintagel, Salisbury, Oxford, and Cambridge. If I'm good enough, I might very well like to study at Cambridge someday. But that depends on which university you're at then.

When I was sitting in Tintagel on a cliff above "Merlin's Cave," I had to think about the knights of the Round Table and the quest for the Holy Grail. According to English legend, only Sir Galahad was allowed to see the Grail and hold it in his hands, and maybe even drink out of it, I'm not sure about that. But afterward he died. I think that must mean that no living person can completely possess the Grail, that is, the chalice from which Jesus drank at the Last Supper, the symbol of love, God's glory, and communion with Jesus. Only when we are dead are we allowed to experience "the truth," only then are we capable of extinguishing the evil within us. Then we are at the end of the quest for . . . well, for the "Holy Grail." (As the legend puts it.) But I believe that a true philosopher is not completely satisfied with pure belief alone!

Now about the discussion in the café.

You know, I actually liked best the opinions of Hans Jonas, Gottfried, and the seventh man at the door to the café.

But somehow none of them is wholly convincing. I shouldn't really say that, since I have found no better solution (maybe I still will). But all the same!

If, as Jakob and Hegel said, good and evil are included within God, then all our human hopes would come to nothing. Then there would also be no Paradise! Then we couldn't fight against evil, because then we would be separating ourselves from God! (But maybe the synthesis doesn't absolutely have to contain evil as well, because if, as Hegel—I think—says, every synthesis gives rise to a new antithesis and then another synthesis, and so on, then it swings back and forth higher and higher and over time the proportion of evil steadily diminishes. Then wouldn't the "limit-synthesis" still consist only of good?)

Zarathustra's explanation is the simplest and maybe even the most convincing. But you already know that I don't believe in an anti-god either! I already wrote something about that in my last letter.

Jonas's view appeals to me. And, you know, I found one of his implied questions particularly interesting. "I much prefer a God who is not omnipotent to a God who does evil." Does God have to be omnipotent?

But best of all I liked Gottfried from Hanover! Maybe good can only exist together with evil, otherwise good would not be recognizable at all!—

No, now I'm getting a queasy feeling—I believe such reasonable claims only lead us farther away from the real truth! Maybe we can approach God only with our hearts. The God in whom I believed in a year ago is suddenly so far away!

All these explanations only make us sad; and God is never conceived as a father or a mother. You don't have to ask many questions about Him! He is simply there, with you!

Sometimes I quarrel with God. Sometimes I'm no longer sure He exists at all.

But fortunately I usually find my way back.—

Incidentally, I finished writing the story about Miriam, and I've already begun to put it on the computer. When it's ready, I'll send it to you, if you like.

I'm already thinking about a new story.

Now I have only one week of vacation left. And I'm spending it with Bettina at a riding school. (My best friend is also coming along.)

And oh, yes—thanks for the card from Denmark! Was it beautiful there? I hope!

In England I read Jane Austen's "Mansfield Park." Do you know Jane Austen? At the moment I'm reading a book about the burning of witches and another that's called "The Czar's Prisoner." You told me once at my age you read the whole Bible all the way through. I think I'll also do that soon!

See you soon, I hope,
Nora

P.S. Please excuse me for having written so messily: I wrote most of this letter in the forest, in Sauerland.

P.P.S. In your letter you used the expression "dead souls." But souls are precisely not dead! They're eternal, aren't they?

Essen, 23 August 1995

Dear Nora,

"Now we're in for it!" —That was my first reaction after a long silence that followed my reading of your letter in the café. General embarrassment reigned until a loud voice was heard. It came from a strict-looking man with a turban, whom I had never seen before.

"Nine hundred years ago I already said that philosophy can only lead to confusion. Philosophers' contradictions are in themselves intolerable when compared with the truth of the heart's revelation, but that a delightful child like Nora, who said perfectly reasonable things about Jesus and who is almost ready to become a virtuous little Muslim, should be confronted by such contradictions, and with the single result that she quarrels with God and is even beginning to doubt His existence—that is simply too much!!! Oh, you philosophers! How good it would be if you didn't exist. You do nothing but damage peoples' souls."

"I am in agreement with much of what you say," replied Blaise (the seventh philosopher from the last time). "Apart, of course, from your comments on Jesus. But you are correct in saying that it is a mistake to think that the question of God can be resolved by reason. Thought's presumption must be humbled, and it is in the humility of the believing heart that we must approach God the Father (and Mother too, so far as I'm concerned!). Philosophy leads nowhere."

"Well, then, the only thing that remains is to close our club," said a third man. "We are declaring not only that we are dead—we've been dead for a long time—we're also declaring that our business is dead. We're entering the post-philosophical age. Hip, hip, hurray!"

"Not so fast, pal," Socrates broke in. "First you have to answer me one little question. Have you any arguments in favor of philosophy's self-dissolution?"

"You're joking, of course? What a question! Of course I have arguments."

"Aren't arguments something philosophical?"

"Yes, certainly."

"But how can we take these arguments seriously—if your point is that arguments, as products of philosophy, can no longer be taken seriously?"

"Stop!" cried a man whom I did not immediately recognize, but who obviously belonged to the Infernal Trio. "Stop right there, Socrates. The argument for the destruction of philosophy was a sort of emetic that empties the stomach, but which then flows away itself."

"Or like a ladder," said another of the band of three, "which you throw away after you've climbed above it."

"But if you do that, don't you fall to the ground?" I asked quite naively.

"Yes," the first speaker replied, "insofar as you don't have an absolute foundation that cannot, of course—and here I agree with the preceding speaker—be provided by philosophy. This foundation is the Koran."

"My dear al-Ghazali, had you not uttered your last sentence . . . well, I'd almost have said you had remained a philosopher, but that only shows the force of habit; I mean, of course, then you would have been right. In truth, the absolute foundation is the Gospel."

"How deplorable that our consensus stops at this point," al-Ghazali answered. "For naturally *your* last assumption is mistaken."

"May I ask another question?" Socrates broke in. "You all wanted to renounce reason because it led to contradictions. But it seems to me that the contradictions among the different religions must not be underestimated. How shall we decide which religion is right?"

"By means of belief, by means of the heart!" al-Ghazali and Blaise cried in unison.

"But you both appeal to belief, and you can't both be right at the same time. How should we decide *which* belief to adopt? By means of belief again? But then our problem arises again, and so on, *ad infinitum*. Or should we perhaps call upon reason to help us?"

A familiar, cackling laughter rang out. A little man with sharp eyes pushed his way forward. It was Tom!

"Hee, hee, hee!" he giggled. "I've got a solution for your problems. Didn't it ever occur to you that most people who are Christians come from Christian countries, whereas most Muslims come—what a coincidence!—from Islamic countries? Ha, ha, ha! What follows from that? Nothing other than this: what people consider true depends on what was hammered into them during their early childhoods."

"Truth is a function of social training," agreed the Viennese man in the Trio. "Ultimate questions are decided as they are generally decided in the society in general."

"You seem to me very clever," Socrates interrupted. "Most philosophers have always maintained that truth is something that precedes social power and in accord with which justly exercised power has to proceed; you, however, have understood that truth ultimately depends on power. My heartiest congratulations on this deep insight!"

"Thanks, thanks," Tom cried with excitement. "Have I now persuaded you as well?"

"I'm always a bit slow, and moreover I've no opinion myself; instead, I want to learn from others. But tell me one thing, Tom: your thesis regarding the precedence of power over truth is your own discovery, and is completely unprecedented and original?"

"Yes indeed!" Tom cried. "Finally someone has understood what I mean!"

"So, your thesis that fundamental truths are hammered into us— did you work that out by yourself?"

"Certainly, and I had to overcome many of my society's prejudices—prejudices that are so strong that even today not everyone, in fact only a few, have understood how great I am."

"That's really too bad, Tom. But tell me just one more thing, before I adopt your view: how could *you* manage to free yourself from the prejudices drilled into you when you were a child? And how can what you say be true, if truth is nothing other than the dominant opinion?"

"I don't understand your question."

"Really? But you're so clever! Let's run through your thesis again. You and Ludwig claimed that there was no possibility of resolving ultimate questions by means of reason. Truth, you said, is whatever one is brought up to believe."

"Precisely!"

"Now the greatness of your mind is shown in the fact that you came to this new insight all by yourself, and were not brought up to believe it. But if you are right, that means that your insight is not the truth."

"Well, I just have to persuade the majority that I'm right—and then I'll be right, too!"

"Tell me, Tom, if you want to persuade someone, do you tell him at the outset that the point for you is that he agree with you, because then your view will become true? Or have you noticed that it is more persuasive to say that one ought to consider something true because it is true, rather than making it true by considering it to be true?"

"Yes, there are people you have to deal with that way, precisely because they are stupid and have not yet recognized the truth!"

"Stupid? Without knowing the truth? How can that be? They make the truth!"

"Socrates, it's impossible to talk with you. You're a sophist and you twist people's words around," Tom replied angrily, and he stalked off. I found Socrates' arguments very good, and I asked him what he thought of Nora's development.

"Well, on the whole it's not so serious. A little doubt does no harm. On the contrary: by passing through doubt Nora will come to a deeper conception of God. Her father and mother won't always be there; someday they will die. To that extent the notion of God as Father or Mother is misleading. God is much more like the truth, which cannot be disputed, because it is presupposed by any dispute. His greatness is shown precisely by the fact that we are brought back to Him like a boomerang whenever we move away from Him. And it is mere thoughtlessness if we don't find our way back to Him."

"I hope you're right, Socrates," al-Ghazali and Blaise cried. "And anyway, our differences are minor compared with those that separate us both from Tom. Let's shake hands! And if the post-philosophical age means clearing the way for people like Tom, then we'd rather put up with you, Socrates!"

"So, the club will not be dissolved, then?" I asked with relief.

"No!" they all cried (including Tom), "there's still far too much to discuss!"

I was satisfied with this answer, and I hope you are, too.

See you soon,
Vittorio

Dear Vittorio,

That was an exciting letter you sent me! Excuse me for not having answered it earlier, but I always have so much to do. We now have many new teachers, and I am getting along well with all of them. In addition, my class went to Sauerland together. We spent three days there in a youth hostel. One day we hiked 26 kilometers around an incredibly beautiful, natural drinking-water lake, through forests and meadows, over little brooks—that is, through Sauerland. From time to time we took little breaks, of course. Once we were given a piece of paper with questions addressed to God, but also to us. We had to answer these questions and then put the paper in an envelope. In two or three years we'll open the envelopes and see what we wrote and thought "then," and discuss it. Neat idea, don't you think?"

At the moment I'm sitting in our cottage in Sauerland again. It's rainy and a little misty, dreary—but I like that. You are probably already in America, since we tried to phone you yesterday, but there was no answer.

Now for your letter.

To Socrates:

Dear Socrates, thanks for having saved the club! I would not have liked it at all if you had dissolved yourselves. Philosophy is very important, even if it has its dangers. Philosophy can sometimes cause you to "lose" your heart or become too "reasonable." (But maybe then it's no longer philosophy, because "philosophy" means "love of truth," and in order to love you need a heart.) And if you only think and think and think and don't participate in real life, that's not good, either.

But I don't believe that philosophy will ever really be abandoned, because we human beings are continually drawn to questions, often passionately. And I like philosophy so much—I'd just think it was stupid if it no longer existed. Then people would have a feeling of emptiness, and that is worse than doubt concerning so many questions and thoughts and reason. You know, recently it sometimes happens that I'm a little melancholy and sad and feel lonely. But usually that quickly goes away.

---

10 October 1995

Dear Vittorio,

Now I'm going to write a little more. First, about Hobbes's theory that power and society are decisive for truth. That's hard, since for human beings environment, customs, and "benefit" are also important to explain a given kind of behavior and to consider it right, for example, religions. But I also believe in an objective truth that is valid for everyone. Maybe one doesn't exclude the other. What is crucial is that human beings' various traditions and customs are changeable and bound up with their time, whereas objective truth is eternal and timeless.

And maybe this is how it is: As little children all people are really "alike." But when we get bigger, we are brought up according to our parents' traditions. Then we begin to search for the truth, the eternal truth, and our search is influenced by the traditions in which we have been brought up (as I said). But if we want to, we can cast off those traditions, because we human beings are free here on earth, because of our reason. However, I believe that we can never cast off the eternal truth, or God. Or rather we can, but I believe that there is nonetheless always a little spark of God within us that we can never completely extinguish. Although that may often not be at all clear to us.

But you know, the idea that the truth has to come from the person who holds power, that's really too silly!

If a father reigns over his family and forbids his wife to take a job, merely because he has the power to do so—does that make it true? Or for example in the time of the witch-hunts—was it right to burn thousands of women because people thought they were possessed by demons? Was that the unique truth? No, unfortunately traditions and customs often go wrong because we don't make enough use of our reason and our hearts.—

In the book I'm reading right now—it's called "Jonathan Blum's Strange Trip Around the World"—there's also a boy, a young Jewish boy, who at the age of seventeen leaves his parents' house and his religion (or tries to) and travels into the wide world in order to find freedom. I have not yet finished it, but it's very good. I got it for my birthday. My birthday was wonderful! So now I'm thirteen. That seems strange, somehow. Oh, well. I also got other books: "The Wonderful Course of Things: The Life of Matthias Claudius," "Wuthering Heights" by Emily Brontë, and "Damascus Nights" by Rafik Schami. They all seem to me to be very good. In addition, I got a drawing-pad and colored pencils, because at the moment I really like drawing. A backpack, new clothes, 2 CDs, and a set-square were also among my presents. I would also have liked to go on a long camping trip with my cousins, who love to sleep out in the open air.

Johannes came to visit on my birthday. I discussed the problem of truth and God with him again—and finally he didn't have any real arguments left! He acted as though he suspected anything that had to do with God, and so he also found the church service where the confirmands are introduced "ridiculous." It took place on Sunday, that is, on my grandmother's birthday. I wrote the sermon. The theme was "The Indifference Many People Feel Toward the Ten Commandments." On the whole, the service went well.

I'm sitting in my room. My baptismal candleholder is also standing on my birthday table—right next to me. I hope you're having a good time in America!

Hope to see you soon,
Nora

P.S. I'm very happy that the club was not dissolved!

P.P.S. I hope you don't end up going to America for good.

Essen, 13 October 1995

Dear Nora,

It was a real joy to be awakened this morning by the mailman (because I was worn out by my flight, I was sleeping much later than usual), who gave me your letter. It made me very sad not to have been able to be at your house on your birthday, though we'll see each other tomorrow anyway—but let me also send you in writing my very best wishes. In particular, I hope that you will overcome the bouts of melancholy that you mentioned and that are completely normal at your age, and that when you are all grown up you will retain your childhood belief, inevitably in a somewhat different form. You have a clear mind and a noble heart—a combination that is unusual, and therefore all the more valuable, and that is the finest gift God could have given you, and in comparison with which other precious birthday gifts pale.

In addition, my absence at your birthday party has one great advantage. It just happened that on precisely the date of your thirteenth birthday I had to give a lecture in Columbus. You know that I like American universities very much, and once again I was very impressed by the hospitality and the interest in the subject shown by my colleagues and the students. My lecture, which dealt with isolation and intersubjectivity in Heraclitus, Llull, and Nietzsche and the ways in which this problem had been expressed in literature, was criticized by a very intelligent and likeable female colleague, whose name was Leslie, who argued that intersubjectivity, which is discussed poetically by Llull and Nietzsche, is only their *subjective* experience, not something real. The objection struck home, because it was only too justified.

Thinking about it, I was walking back to my hotel, when I noticed a crowd of people involved in a heated discussion on the lawn in a secluded part of the campus.

"The letters are obviously a forgery—a clever forgery, granted, but you can't pull the wool over the eyes of a developmental psychologist like me. An eleven-year-old kid cannot ask such precise questions about the relationship between divine omnipotence and freedom of the will."

"Wait a minute, Jean, you're greatly overestimating your developmental psychology insights," said someone whom I quickly recognized as our old friend Jean-Jacques. "Among compatriots we can speak openly, and I've always thought that you managed to penetrate the thoughts but not the souls of children. Woe to him who seeks to understand the mind without the soul! And woe to the age that promotes the intellect without a cultivation of the emotions. There is no doubt whatever that such questions can proceed from a soul like Nora's . . ."

So they were talking about our birthday girl! Leaning against a tree, I kept quiet and listened to the discussion.

"Tell me, Jean-Jacques, have you ever seen this Nora with your own eyes?"

"No, and that's why I'm so sad. I would have liked very much to be her guardian philosopher, but Giambattista snatched her away from me."

"Well, then! A little critical thinking, please. If the theory asserts that something is impossible and there is no persuasive empirical counterevidence, then it is crazy to resist the theory—or at least it is unscientific, unenlightened . . ."

"The hell with Enlightenment! I *feel* that Nora exists. I don't need to see her with my own eyes. She has already appeared to me several times in my dreams . . ."

"A clear case of projection," said an elderly bearded gentleman with glasses and a Viennese accent. "One to zip for you, Jean. Fortunately, our science makes us somewhat more critical than philosophy."

"Nonetheless, Nora is something like an archetype," interrupted a third man with a strong Swiss accent. "I'd say, Sigmund, that she corresponds to a childlike sibyl, who ought to inspire an aging philosopher."

"Nora is real, Carl Gustav," said an energetic voice from the back of the crowd. "I've seen her with my own eyes—in her city's church one Sunday morning."

"Well, yes, Augustine, perhaps you hadn't slept well. And I'll even gladly concede that you met some young girl or other. But that doesn't prove that she was the author of these questionable letters. Look . . . here in the letter about your meeting (whoever the author is) it says that you are black. But you aren't. Nora (that is, the diabolical creature who is concealed under this name and who clearly has the dastardly intention of leading the science of psychology around by the nose) obviously arrived at that conclusion from reading that you were born in Africa. And you projected all kinds of things into her in turn."

"All the same," Sigmund interrupted Jean, "this intentional naiveté on Nora's part is particularly clever. But no one can fool us. The author simply *presents herself or himself* as naive."

"Excuse me if I break in here," said a friendly-looking man in a bishop's gown, "of course it is conceivable that 'Nora' perceived our friend Augustine as black. Colors are subjective, after all."

"How's that?"

"Well, if 'Nora' describes the English landscape as melancholy, that results either from the fact that she is herself melancholic, or that her inventor wants her to appear melancholic here. But the landscape itself is never, ever melancholic! Thus Augustine is not in himself black—it depends on the constitution of the eyes, or rather, on the soul, of the person to whom he appears."

"Does that hold true only for colors, George?"

"Of course not, it holds for all material things. It exists only through consciousness."

"Through which consciousness, yours? Are we nothing outside your consciousness?"

"I wouldn't go that far . . ."

"But I would! I am the only one who exists and you are my property!"

"Come now, Max, leave us in peace, would you?"

But Max clapped his hands and since he looked pretty disagreeable, I closed my eyes.

When I opened them again, no one was there—including Max. Wasn't Leslie right? Are we philosophers doomed to be prisoners of the immanence of consciousness?

If I compare the reaction of the philosophers to your birthday this year with their reaction last year, three things occur to me. First, the participants were different; second, Naples is a livelier, less critical city than Columbus, and third, thirteen is not so round a number as twelve!

Warmest greetings from
Your Vittorio

Dear Vittorio,

Thanks for the letter you brought with you when you came to see us for the first time in more than a month. I'm sorry that it has gotten so late again and you have had to wait such a long time for an answer.

Vittorio, Mama told me that you want to publish our letters! At first I couldn't really believe it. Publish?! Where? And what if someone I know were to read them? We'll have to talk about it when you come next time.

First, however, about your bewildering letter.

1. Dear psychologists, how much I would have liked to invite you to tea, in order to show you that I exist. (You probably would have thought I was an illusion.) Since I can't do that and still haven't been able to prove that I, Nora, am alive, and wrote the letters to Vittorio, and am thirteen years old, for the present you'll have *believe* me. (But you won't be able to do that.) You say that children can't write such letters; since I did in fact write them, your claim is disproven!

Moreover, I don't believe that adults could write such letters—in many ways we children are ahead of you. For example, children are not as cold and calculating as you are. And I have to agree with Jean-Jacques: "Woe to him who seeks to understand the mind without the soul!"

2. How can the existence of other people be proven? I don't know exactly how, either. But maybe this way: through love and also through hate, and through an exchange of ideas. You can hardly discuss things with a "fantasy." A "fantasy" can give one no real thoughts with which one can come to terms. In addition, real feelings can be shown only for another person.

In addition, we would be—yes, we would be deceived if the world around us didn't exist, wouldn't we?

That holds not only for other people, but also for the whole external world. Do you think that God deceives us? Once you wrote to me: "Perhaps God deceives us about the truth."

What do you think about that? Do you believe that we are deceived regarding our own bodies? I'm not sure what I should think. Earlier I thought that human beings consisted of matter and spirit together, but now I'm no longer so certain. What if the world is a dream? It would be dreadful, inconceivable! But maybe it's this way: our world is not a dream, only it's not our only world, that is, we also live in another world that's invisible.

Sometimes it's as if something were standing in the middle of our world, and I think I'm somewhere else besides here . . .

Oh, this is all so complicated.

3. Hmm, what is subjective and what is objective?

I also believe that the senses are subjective, as George says. In fact, the whole human being is subjective. Each human being is subjective, but he also has something objective in him. It's what binds all people together, but then we are also always an object, when others observe us.

Oh, yes, I finished writing my story. It also has a title now: "His Boat."

Do you think that's appropriate? I'm already thinking about a new story. We'll see; it may turn out to be a Christmas story.

Last weekend we went to Berlin. There we visited friends and went sight-seeing (naturally, we couldn't see everything). I like the French Cathedral very much, but the Berlin Cathedral is horrible! Kitsch, splendor, boastfulness, power—nothing else. It's no House of God, but rather a "house" in which the Kaiser and his relatives wanted to immortalize themselves, something for "show"! Great!

Berlin is a very beautiful city, I think. But I don't know if I'd like to live there someday. In addition, we "visited" our old house. I can still remember a lot about it, since I spent the first three years of my life there. We also saw a ballet, "The Snow Queen," in the opera house. It was wonderful!

Who was this strange Max, anyway? When I jokingly told Bettina that she was my property, that she was my fantasy and in actuality she didn't exist at all, she replied curtly: "Then I'm going to tickle you, and you'll soon see whether I exist!"

The first snow fell today—when it snows it's always so mysteriously quiet. In general, there's something mysterious in the air, now that it's Advent, don't you think?

Right now I'm reading "Gustav Adolph's Page," by Meyer. At the moment I'm suffering from a lack of books. I read "Wuthering Heights"—it's very good. So now I have to get going, to pick you up at the train station.

So I'll see you soon,
Nora

P.S. *Scribo epistolas, ergo sum!*

---

9 December 1995

Dear Nora,

As always, your letter gave me great joy—many thanks! How nice that you saw the city of your birth again. Your remarks on the Berlin Cathedral are right on the mark—if only all people were like you and thought more about God than about their own power, the world would be in better condition. In order to refute many philosophers it suffices to tickle them—you don't need to do anything more than that.

I can well understand that you found my last letter bewildering—these psychologists also struck me as quite strange. What I didn't like about them was that they treated you like an object—they wanted to learn something *about* you, not *from* you. For me, on the contrary, you are always a genuine conversation partner. Therefore it is very important that you make your own decision regarding whether we publish our letters or not.

With your letter and your questions in my head I walked this morning to the famous café. How astounded I was when I read on the door:

"Closed for remodeling." I was nonplussed, and pounded on the closed door: "Let me in, I need a philosopher."

"Take it easy, take it easy, young man!" I suddenly heard a voice say, and an elderly man with a noble face and a long beard shuffled toward the door on the inside, and then unlocked it.

"What's going on here, anyway?" I asked him. "Why is the place being remodeled?"

"Because Nora's mind is changing—but don't worry, after the remodeling everything will be even more beautiful. Come on in."

I sat down at a table and looked more closely at the old man. I was sure that I had never met him before, but his face somehow seemed familiar.

"Do we know each other? Are you a philosopher? Or are you only overseeing the remodeling?"

"The latter, the latter. No, we've never met. But I have heard of Nora, and even met her once."

"What do you think of her?"

"A remarkable kid—or should I already say: young lady?"

"Even if you're not a philosopher, can you help us? Nora is unsure, she no longer knows what's real. She wonders whether God deceives us, and sometimes she even quarrels with God. At night she is tormented by the dream that everything might be only a dream."

"In a certain sense, that's right. The world of our experiences is not the true reality—it is only the imitation of another higher reality. And only if we rise to this sphere can we answer the question whether other people exist, whether matter exists, and so on."

"But people argue about whether there is a higher world; some even doubt the existence of God. However, only a few odd philosophers have questioned the existence of the everyday world."

"They may be odd, but they are right. The world of experience *seems* to us to be more real than any possible other one. But in truth this other world *is* of a higher level, and it is also more profoundly knowable. Only if we raise ourselves to the ideal world—and that is God—do we see the empirical world in the right light. Only because we know that God wants there to be a plurality of human beings, because morality is realized in the relationships among them, can we be certain that other people exist—if we just analyze our consciousness, we cannot get beyond it. Only because we know that the spirit of the world has to free itself from what lacks spirit, can we be sure that there is a nature independent of consciousness—of course, only as the presupposition of the spirit's development."

"That sounds interesting. But can you also explain the proposition that Descartes once formulated here: 'Perhaps God deceives us about the truth'?"

"That's not hard. God can only will the truth, and thus He can only lead us toward it, insofar as we don't resist it. But He can deceive us insofar as He does so within the sphere of the empirical."

"How is that?"

"Well, think of art. Did the stories that Nora has just written really happen?"

"No, presumably not."

"So is our little friend a liar?"

"Listen, old man, I know hardly anyone who is so concerned with the truth as Nora is."

"That's what I think, too. But she does like to write stories, and what she writes does not occur in reality. Therefore she deceives us!"

"No, you pig-headed old man! She only wants to lead us toward deeper truths."

"So she deceives us about the truth—just like God. Artists are friends of truth and deceivers at the same time—that's what makes them so fascinating. This proposition can be understood only if we distinguish between empirical and ideal reality. If we do that, then we can correctly understand what happens in art, and Nora is as talented as a philosopher as she is as a writer."

"Say, old man, what you're telling me reminds me a little of Plato. He has always been my favorite philosopher, and I'm very sad that I have never met him here in the café. Does he come so seldom? Frankly, however, in the end I'm also glad of that, because all the other philosophers intimidated me, but if I met him, the greatest of them all, just like that, I might die of awe."

"I know," said the old man, with an enchanting smile, "and that's why I didn't introduce myself at the outset . . ."

I stared at him. "Are you Plato?"

I fainted, and when I came to, Plato was gone, the café had melted away, I was sitting in your workroom, and you were just coming back from school. Yes, and so I can only give you this letter.

In constant friendship,
Your Vittorio

Dear Nora,

I want to write *you* the first letter of the new year (by hand, of course, since I don't have a computer here), so that you don't get the impression that I want to break off our correspondence. On the contrary, I hope you'll write back soon! As you know, your letters are particularly important to me, and I am certain that our (letter) friendship will continue all our lives. We inevitably and fortunately change throughout our lives, but something, which provides the foundation of this transformation, remains intact. As your mother told me, you had a very nice Christmas day and now you are seeing in the new year in Sauerland. I hope you have all gotten a good rest and gathered strength for the new year.

On New Year's eve I went walking along the Danube, gazing thoughtfully into the water. Suddenly I noticed that someone was looking at me, and turned around.

"The flow of water reminds one of the flow of time, doesn't it?" asked a man whom the dark made unrecognizable.

"Certainly, but now at the end of the year, it seems as though there were sharp breaks in the flow of time, retroactive changes, so to speak, whereas the water here flows so regularly and uniformly. That's a difference, anyway."

"Yes, but that is true only for *our* perception of time—individuals' and society's perception of time—not for time in itself. In a few hours things won't happen as they did yesterday and the day before, even if suddenly the fireworks are ignited—yet time itself flows on in as leisurely a manner as ever."

"But why does our perception of time differ from time in itself?"

"Well, because we are more interesting than time is. We have a task—and therefore we have to change. Becoming old and even dying is a privilege of the higher levels of being. In stones, time flows as something external, in organic beings it is internalized to a certain extent. Human beings, after all, know about time, and about death. They are the most temporal of all beings; their being is saturated with temporality."

"And yet human beings are capable of knowing the world of ideas, and it is timeless."

"Yes, that's true. We human beings are both the most time-bound and the most timeless beings—more temporal than stones and animals, yet at the same time timeless."

"That sounds mysterious."

"And it is, too. And many other things depend on this mystery."

"Which ones?"

"Well, that we grow old, change, but at the same time come nearer to the timeless: growing up is both—raising oneself toward the timeless world, and simultaneously an increase in temporality."

"But I am not the only one who changes—my fellow human beings also change, and they may change in a different way, because they are older or younger."

"Right. The world of relationships among human beings, and not only our own stream of consciousness, is saturated with temporality. That is exciting, but it also creates problems."

"Such as?"

"Well, every teaching relationship presupposes a difference in lived time between the teacher and the pupil. The former is older, the latter younger."

"Education is so difficult. On one hand education can be distinguished from training only if the pupil to be educated is taken seriously as fully human, and on the other hand there is an inequality based on the greater age of the teacher, without which we can't speak of education at all. How can one reconcile the two?"

"All interesting tasks consist in harmoniously reconciling two apparently opposed elements. Didn't we begin by saying that human beings combine in a wonderful way both temporality and timelessness? Such a harmony between autonomy and asymmetry must also occur in education."

"Tell me, stranger," I interrupted him there, "how I should handle the following situation. The year that is presently coming to a close and the preceding year were marked by a marvelous exchange of letters with a little girl-philosopher . . ."

"The famous Dino-Nora," he interrupted, "who doesn't know about her? And I also know what your problem is. Your correspondence was a mutual opportunity in which you learned a great deal *from* Nora. But then you have read many books about children's philosophy, and all these educationists and psychologists only want to learn *about* children, not *from* them. Thereby, however, the children are reduced to objects, and you have also done that when you rise to the meta-level and begin to reflect on her development. Indeed, you've even objectified yourself, since shortly before your text on Nora you also wrote an essay about your own development, in which you observed yourself from outside, so to speak. But you are older than Nora, and I think it's easier to observe one's own development—even if Nora's guardian philosopher once discussed her development with me."

"What should I do, then, in the coming year?"

"Very simple: on the meta-level, that is, the level of reflection on the development of your exchange of letters, reestablish equality. Ask Nora how *she* sees her development, what she likes or dislikes in your exchange of letters and in your text. But don't push her to answer quickly—she has a lot to do, and even though she's still young, her manifold duties are still time-consuming."

Then the stranger rose into the air, and I recognized—Giambattista! His guardian philosopher's wings rustled in the wind and I could still hear them when the New Year's cannons began to sound.

"Happy New Year!" he called to me, "to you—and to Nora! She will make further progress in philosophy, I'm sure; I only want her to be near you. At your age one doesn't develop much more; therefore it's much more interesting to be a thirteen-year-old's guardian philosopher!"

And he disappeared. But I am writing you this letter.

As ever,
Your Vittorio

Childhood and Philosophy

An Afterword by Vittorio Hösle

> Thou, whose exterior semblance doth belie
> Thy Soul's immensity;
> Thou best Philosopher, who yet dost keep
> Thy heritage, thou Eye among the blind,
> That, deaf and silent, read'st the eternal deep,
> Haunted for ever by the eternal mind,—
> Mighty Prophet! Seer blest!
> On whom those truths do rest,
> Which we are toiling all our lives to find,
> In darkness lost, the darkness of the grave;
> Thou, over whom thy immortality
> Broods like the Day, a Master o'er a Slave,
> A Presence which is not to be put by;
> Thou little Child, yet glorious in the might
> Of heaven-born freedom on thy being's height,
> Why with such earnest pains dost thou provoke
> The years to bring the inevitable yoke,
> Thus blindly with thy blessedness at strife?
> Full soon thy Soul shall have her earthly freight,
> And custom lie upon thee with a weight,
> Heavy as frost, and deep almost as life!

> William Wordsworth,
> *Ode: Intimations of Immortality from*
> *Reflections of Early Childhood, VIII*

There are many good books about philosophizing with children.[1] In addition, two German scholarly journals have devoted special issues to children's philosophy,[2] and in the United States there is even a journal devoted to this topic.[3] There is also no lack of books on philosophy that are suitable for children: Jostein Gaarder's *Sophie's World*[4] has recently become a worldwide best-seller, even if its readers may include more adults than children. What is new, and perhaps unique, about the present work is that it contains the philosophy *of* a child.

This novelty seems to justify publishing an exchange of letters that is actually private in nature, though there were many arguments for not publishing it. My goal is not to make available objectivizing materials for developmental psychology, but rather to encourage children—and perhaps also adults—to philosophize as uninhibitedly as Nora does. If in the following pages there is a change of roles, and Nora's correspondent, not without a certain uneasiness, expresses his views as a professional philosopher regarding the problem of children's philosophy, he does so only in order to allow readers to put these letters into a larger context to which they can feel that they themselves belong.

In what follows, a few general, that is, philosophical, considerations regarding the relationship between philosophy and childhood will first be set forth; secondly, some empirical data on this relationship will be reported; thirdly, the child who wrote what is doubtless the more important half of the correspondence will be introduced. The analysis of these letters will be followed by a few brief reflections on the problem of children's talents and on the role of philosophy in education.

I.

Isn't the concept of children's philosophy a *contradictio in adiecto*? Aren't childhood and philosophy conceivable only as far removed from one another? On one hand we have a time of life marked by pleasure in play, by imagination, and by naiveté; on the other a branch of knowledge that is marked by serious, abstract conceptuality and reflection—what elements could be farther removed from each other? However, in truth the relationships between them are so close than we can definitely say that those who have failed to preserve some characteristic traits of childhood within themselves are not well-suited to practice philosophy.

First of all, childhood and philosophy have in common their wonder at the world. For children, the world is not old hat; it awakens their curiosity. The constant questions that children start asking when still very young are a sign of the determination of the human mind to find order in the world, to discover relationships, to solve puzzles. The why-question itself points to the relationship between philosophy and childhood. Of course, the competence to answer many of the child's why-questions is to be found in the various individual branches of knowledge, but that doesn't hold for all questions; indeed, the teleological orientation that is often implicit in the child's "why" alongside the causal meaning suffices to indicate an original philosophical need. If the child wants to know why we die, he or she is not primarily interested in a list of the causes of death—the child wants to know about the possible meaning of death.[5] For that very reason, children's questions are generally related to a point of unity— for the child, the individual problems are connected, as they are in philosophy, which may be able to unite the ever-increasing plenitude of the branches of knowledge into a cosmos.

To be sure, we can justifiably dismiss the importance of many questions children ask—understanding that some questions are illegitimate is an important philosophical step forward. Moreover, further progress in knowledge would not be possible if we did not set aside certain issues, abstain from analyzing them, and content ourselves with the usual, generally accepted views. But it is of the utmost importance to recognize that this setting aside is preliminary and a sign of our weakness, rather than a special achievement. So far as unjustified questions are concerned, they are much less to be deplored than the kind of philosophy that declares (as do logical positivism and hermeneutics, for instance) that any question it cannot answer is illegitimate. Similarly, adults err when they ironically dismiss fundamental questions asked in all earnestness by children, merely because they themselves cannot answer them or because they are afraid of the consequences of the right answer. In so doing they injure the soul of the child, who is willing to be guided by the adult, but can always tell when the adult is unfairly exploiting his superior power. Indeed, they endanger the child's spiritual development, in which conversations with patient interlocutors are particularly important—for not all children have the inner strength not to be deterred from seeking to satisfy their curiosity and thirst for knowledge, despite all the disappointments that proceed from their apparently superior elders.

However, the bridge between childhood and philosophy is not built of wonder and curiosity alone. Even the three marks of childhood mentioned above—pleasure in play, imagination, and naiveté—cannot be forfeited by a philosopher without great damage. So far as play is concerned, it is ridiculous to oppose it to seriousness. Anyone who has seen how children play knows that a great deal of concentration goes into play, as into any activity that is viewed both as an end in itself and as bound by specific rules whose observance is regarded as an absolute moral duty. Aren't these views applicable to philosophy as well? Didn't Plato, in the *Laches,* describe Socrates' philosophizing as a kind of elevated wrestling match, as pleasurable, as an activity that was practiced for its own sake and at the same time rule-governed and morally valuable?

Present-day philosophy provides ample evidence that without imagination philosophy is doomed to failure. To be sure, philosophy has to be restrained, ideas have to be criticized, and for that purpose abstract concepts and logic are absolutely necessary. However, logical criticism can only be brought to bear when ideas are already on the table; it cannot produce these ideas itself. Heuristics precedes criticism, and without constructive imagination, system-building, for instance, is completely impossible. In short, philosophy needs not to eliminate but to supervise imagination.

Finally, naiveté is absolutely indispensable for substantive philosophizing. In Hans Christian Andersen's fable, it is only a child who can cry out that the emperor has no clothes. However, the philosopher—resisting all the prejudices of his own time and his own situation—must also be capable of seeing what is actually there, in its immediacy, even if doing so involves a breach of etiquette.[6] To be sure, reflection, that is, turning away from the world and turning toward one's own activity, is also an important philosophical method that first emerges in late childhood or adolescence. But firstly, reflection presupposes a previously existing relationship to an object, if it is not to turn in empty circles within itself, and secondly, philosophical reflection must be distinguished from the pure self-absorption that constitutes the chief malady of modern humanity—philosophical reflection is concerned with general acts, not with individual moods. To that extent we can speak of objective reflection, and we can conceive of a philosopher for whom the reflective attitude has become completely natural and who proceeds in it with complete naiveté and childlike security.

II.

However, abstract considerations will not convince us that child-hood is a time of life that is, or at least can be, particularly favorable to philosophy. The claim also has to be proven empirically. Long before child and adolescent psychology were developed as an independent discipline in this century, countless important authors have described how as children and adolescents they were tormented by questions that have traditionally been dealt with—though at a higher level of abstraction—by philosophy. Epicurus, for example, wrote that when he was fourteen he had begun to take an interest in philosophy.[7] Many great thinkers have begun constructing their systems in their twenties, and sometimes even in their teens, even if it usually took them a long time to work out their initial intuitions, and this suggests that as children they were already ruminating on metaphysical issues. Particularly interesting in this regard is the report of a writer whose work constantly raises abstract philosophical questions and who is nonetheless at the same time, by a rare combination, one of the most illustrious realists of all time. Count Leo Tolstoy's trilogy *Childhood— Boyhood—Youth* (which he originally planned as a tetralogy, but the last volume was never written), his first publication, is not an auto-biography in the strict sense of the term. However, the first-person narrator Nikolenka Irtenjew has so many of Tolstoy's characteristics that his thoughts and feelings can certainly be attributed to the young writer.

In the nineteenth chapter of *Boyhood,* Tolstoy describes young Nikolenka's unconventional thoughts. Right at the beginning of *Boy-hood,* which deals with the period from about nine to sixteen years of age, in the third chapter ("A New View"), a radical change in the boy's way of thinking is represented. Traveling toward Moscow, he sud-denly realizes the importance of differences in status and wealth, indeed, in a very basic way, that his family is not the center of the world, and that there are other people who know nothing about him and his family and have nothing to do with them. In connection with this basic recognition, the world suddenly seems to turn toward him a different, previously unknown side.[8] However, a new sphere appears not only outside the family; young Nikolenka also becomes increasingly isolated within the family. In retrospect, his boyhood looks like a "desert,"[9] because it was a time without the warm feelings that enriched his childhood and later poetically enchanted his youth.

During this period of isolation, Nikolenka thought about things that were hardly suited to his age and situation—"I think, however, that the incongruity of a man's situation with his moral activity is the surest proof of his sincerity."[10] Tolstoy cites the topos (which goes back to antiquity) according to which the development of the individual corresponds to the development of the species, and uses it to explain why during his boyhood he was already engaged in philosophical thinking. Nikolenka imagines that he is the first to have discovered these truths, although the accompanying sense of self-worth does not succeed in overcoming his shyness in dealing with others—on the contrary. Among the boy's discoveries are the insight that happiness is subjective and depends not on things, but on our relationship to them, the awareness of the omnipresence of death, the recognition of the meaning of symmetries (from which Nikolenka tries to conclude that there must be not only a life after death but also a life before birth), and finally the solipsistic suspicion that things only exist when he is observing them. "There were moments when I became so deranged by this *idée fixe* that I would glance sharply round in some opposite direction, hoping to catch unawares the void (the *néant*) where I was not."[11]

What is fascinating about this behavior is the contradiction between the level of the questions and the inadequacy of the means of answering them. In fact, we have to acknowledge that children may well be unable to deal with the issues they inquire into. Tolstoy himself did not look back with pleasure on the philosophical efforts of his youth—he laments a loss in natural feeling and a tendency toward an endless series of reflections, even when in 1909–1910, shortly before his death, he represented, in the dialogues entitled "Childlike Wisdom," philosophizing children who are often wiser than adults. Tolstoy is not the only one who sees dangers in premature philosophizing—Giambattista Vico, who was perhaps the first (several decades before Rousseau) to grasp the uniqueness and special worth of childlike thinking, deplores the fact that he was made to study logic too soon. According to him, this overtaxing of his young mind, which was not yet accustomed to abstractions, caused him to interrupt his studies for a year and a half,[12] during which time he had to call upon and develop his childish imagination and his memory. Schopenhauer, without knowing Vico, promotes similar conceptions,[13] correctly seeing a danger in the common practice of having children talk about things they have not really understood. A loss of the spontaneous capacity for experience, technical overtaxing, and finally and ultimately precociousness, are in fact among the risks that accompany an excessively early concern with philosophy, and therefore it is hardly surprising that children's philosophy in general is regarded with skepticism.

Thus we constantly hear that while children may be able to ask philosophical questions, it is obvious that they cannot answer them, and that they should therefore not be encouraged to entertain philosophical ideas, if not actively discouraged from doing so. This conviction is often based on ontogenetic evolutionism, according to which certain intellectual achievements first become possible at a certain age. Thus modern developmental psychology, particularly since the path-breaking work of Jean Piaget,[14] has sought to show that a child first becomes capable of formal operations at the age of eleven or twelve, and that such operations can be mastered only starting with the fourth phase of the development of the intelligence—after the sensory-motor phase of early infancy, the pre-operative phase from one-and-one-half to seven, and the phase of concrete operations from seven to eleven. (Piaget divides individual phases into various stages.) In fact, one of the most significant and bewildering discoveries made by psychology in this century is that children cannot answer certain questions that seem to us elementary. To a question that can be answered by means of simple logical reflection, such as whether there are more birds or pigeons, an eight-year-old still cannot usually give the right answer, because the totality of birds and pigeons is not given in visible form. Perceiving contradictions, seeing through circular reasoning, and other similar operations are not self-evident—only in puberty do young people learn to master them. Even simpler concrete operations cannot be carried out by a pre-school child—duration and speed seem to children to be directly, not indirectly proportional magnitudes: they think that if they move with greater speed—run, for instance—it will take them longer than if they move slowly.[15]

The empirical results of developmental psychology—which are important as well, especially for the ontogenesis of moral thought—are, if not exactly uncontested, at least generally recognized, and their philosophical significance is not in doubt. Naturally, the phase of formal operations represents an advance over the preceding phases. Anyone who seeks to conclude, from the fact that people of differing ages or cultures think differently, that all forms of thought are equally legitimate, is committing an error, because he is contradicting himself: he fails to see that the meta-position he adopts is only one position among others, and therefore, according to his own mode of argument, must also be relativized. Evolutionism is correct in principle, and in fact the child himself recognizes that he has to learn from adults. However, ontogenetic and phylogenetic evolutionism becomes one-sided and dangerous when it can no longer recognize that the earlier phases may be in other respects superior to the later ones. Thus primitiveness in the sense of originality is always ahead of the more developed phases in some way—in the freshness of its approach to the world. We never again learn so much or so quickly as in our first year and a half, and even an eleven-year-old child can still ask questions of a profundity that the adult, with his advanced instruments of knowledge, would do well to seek to answer. As already said, logic is not a method for approaching essential questions, and yet the quality of the answers depends among other things on the quality of the questions.[16] In the history of philosophy one can hardly speak of a continuous progress, either—the structural clarity of Gorgias's work on nonbeing compensates for its logical fallacies. Still clearer is the one-sidedness of an approach to art that emphasizes only its progress. The discovery of perspective incontestably represents an important achievement in the history of painting, but that does not mean that precisely in periods of excessive refinement recourse to "more primitive" forms of representation may not be fruitful, or even the sole possible way of overcoming stagnation and imitativeness. Basically, the constantly renewed confrontations with the childlike worldview may be, on one hand, historically earlier, archaic forms of consciousness, and on the other hand one of the most powerful antidotes against the loss of spontaneity and immediacy that threatens later ages in life and periods in history alike.

The dangers to which philosophizing with children is exposed must not be underestimated, but neither can we ignore the basic philosophical questions that spring forth with elemental power in many children and that so clearly demonstrate that philosophical wonder is an anthropological constant, an original human need. What should we do then? The best reaction to the aforementioned dilemma seems to me the following: we approach children's questions in all seriousness while trying, firstly, to avoid all abstract questions that can be approached only by means of logical operations for which children are not yet ready. Secondly, since precociousness is a defect, we must take care that the issues with which children concern themselves are rooted in their lifeworlds. An adult who philosophizes with children must not spell out in advance answers that children can only take in, but not really understand; rather, he must ask counter-questions that lead the child to move in the right direction and, if possible, to feel his way toward the answers by himself. There is no philosophy without autonomous insight, even if it would be the greatest error of abstract explanation to believe that autonomy is achieved over-night rather than being the complex result of a transmission of a tra-dition that offers itself even as it withdraws. Fairies are no less part of a child's lifeworld than are cars; therefore, thirdly, it may be helpful to translate the fascination characteristic of philosophy into the lan-guage of imagination, which is the child's proper idiom. It is perhaps no surprise that Parmenides, the founder of Western logic, introduces his main work with a description of a journey to see a goddess who re-veals the truth to him, but even the father of modern science, Des-cartes, attributed great significance to the three dreams he had on the eve of St. Martin's, 1619, which followed an important scientific discovery. However, children have a right to expect that we clothe philosophy in the world of imagination. Fourthly, it is crucial that the child's philosophizing not take place completely alone. Certainly, loneliness is often a painful but nonetheless unavoidable condition of the possibility of creativity; but if phases of lonely reflection do not al-ternate with phases of dialogue, then the danger arises that the child will wither and turn away from other children of his age. Philosophiz-ing is more than the art of carrying on a conversation, but dialogue is a particularly appropriate framework for philosophizing, because it makes one familiar with a variety of positions that one cannot simply dogmatically reject, but rather has to think through before one either accepts them or immanently denies them.

On the basis of these principles there has been, for at least ten years, an intensive practice of children's philosophy. Whereas the rubric "Philosophy" is not to be found in the German scholar Ch. Bühler's classic work, *Kindheit und Jugend,*[17] the American research-ers Matthew Lipman (the founder of his own institute for the pro-motion of philosophy for children) and Gareth B. Matthews, both of whom are internationally-known representatives of this approach, begin from the conviction that philosophizing is a basic need of chil-dren, and should be met along with needs such as physical activity and music. These two investigators conduct conversations with groups of children that constantly move around philosophical questions,

Lipman giving the more formal problems priority, and Matthews the more content-oriented problems.[18] Their writings are partly philosophical texts for children and partly elaborations on their experiences with children. In Germany, Hans-Ludwig Freese, a professor of education, has promoted the practice and theory of children's philosophy.

III.

Gaarder's *Sophie's World* had an influence on the young girl who wrote the letters contained in this book that was similar to the tutor's influence on Molière's Monsieur Jourdain: just as the latter learned to his amazement that he had spoken prose all his life without knowing that he was doing so, Nora learned by reading Gaarder's book, which was given her on her eleventh birthday, that many of the questions she had already long thought about could be described as "philosophical," and that a whole series of illustrious thinkers had already grappled with them. Shortly before, I had met the young girl for the first time at her home. It was friendship at first sight, and I believe that the mutual understanding that arose between us was partly due to a question I asked her immediately after we were introduced— whether she had been named after Ibsen's heroine. She was not able to answer the question by herself, because the name Ibsen meant nothing to her, but she ran to her parents and came back a short while later with shining eyes and gave me an affirmative answer. She was obviously excited to learn for the first time why she was named "Nora" (no doubt a bit of information relevant to her identity), and she curiously inquired about the literary figure, for whom she immediately felt admiration.

At the end of the year 1993, a problem began to concern Nora. In Gaarder's book, she had learned about Plato's doctrine of the Ideas, and it had made a great impression on her. However, a critical question was bothering her: what about the Platonic idea of dinosaurs? Ideas were timeless and therefore could not pass away; but the dinosaurs had died out long ago. Did the idea of dinosaurs still exist all the same? It didn't take much of a talent scout to see that this child, who had come to this question all by herself, was philosophically gifted, and after I had given her on the telephone an explanation that satisfied her for the moment, I sent her a dinosaur made of marzipan (here

I should mention that Nora had never taken an interest in the dinosaur fad that followed Spielberg's film *Jurassic Park*). Her thank-you note showed not only an astonishing sense of ideal as opposed to material value (the marzipan dinosaur was never eaten), but also expressed annoyance with Aristotle's image of women as it had been presented in school. Here we see one of Nora's characteristic traits: despite her admiration for the great figures of intellectual history, her sense of justice does not allow her to avoid seeing their weaknesses. Her card seemed to me to require an extended reply; my first letter was followed by a long answer from Nora, out of which the correspondence published here eventually grew, and was constantly complemented by conversations in person and on the telephone.

Reading Nora's letters, a lay psychologist and pedagogue is struck by a clear break. The first twenty letters are marked by a very lively imagination; the first ones are even accompanied by drawings. Nora describes her encounters with the great philosophers in an extremely vivid manner; every line breathes joy in life, trust in God, love of nature. The argumentative level is unusually high: one has only to read her explanation of why my encounters in the café cannot have all taken place in a dream. However, the context in which her train of thought is developed is particularly remarkable—she does not want to put in question the reality of the café of the dead but eternally young philosophers. Naturally she is well aware that this café does not have the same degree of reality as the pizzeria across the street; but she is convinced that anything that has an inner truth has a higher and not a lesser degree of reality than the empirical world. In this conviction, the child and the archaic human being are perhaps even nearer the true facts of the matter than the prosaic thinker of the disenchanted world. When Nora read in an encyclopedia that for Wittgenstein the world is all that is the case, she said, "But then every mystery is destroyed." From her belief in the reality of the café emerges Nora's hunger for concreteness: when she read that Giambattista Vico had won out over Jean-Jacques Rousseau and been appointed as her guardian philosopher, she asked her mother who had made this decision, how it had been arrived at, and so on.

It's marvelous how she combines the wish to be guided with a strong will to autonomy. The first letter is already a small masterpiece in this regard. In my quickly dashed-off letter I had referred, taking my inspiration from the film *Dead Poets Society*, to the café of the dead but ever young philosophers (*das Café der toten, aber ewig jungen Philosophen*), but she corrected the strange name—independently and without in any way emphasizing what she had done—to read "the café of the philosophers who have died, but are ever young" (*das Café der gestorbenen, aber ewig jungen Philosophen*)—and she was fully justified in doing so, because *tot* indicates a more final, ultimate condition than does *gestorben*. Also noteworthy is the fact that Plato tells her that she must discover the address of this café by herself. This announcement contains a demand for independence, but it comes precisely from Plato, an adult authority—and of course the meeting with him is her own invention. We could speak here of self-education, insofar as Nora creates her own models, and then uses them as guides. No less remarkable is the fact that Nora begins the whole correspondence with a reflection on her role as a woman—a reflection that is followed later by thoughts on herself as a child. But while she herself recognizes that as a child she still has much to learn, and does not understand the significance of children for answering Nietzsche's questions, the oppression of women outrages her very deeply—and she replaces Father Christmas with Mother Christmas. In the course of our correspondence Nora becomes more independent. In March 1995, for instance, she reports her flight to the café (even if only to its courtyard), toward which she is moving, as she told me repeatedly with great emphasis. However, up to now she has not yet entered it.

It is fascinating how Nora is able to respond to her conversation and correspondence partner. The fact that she had written to me about Anaximander, after I had alluded to him using a Greek word, strikes her as remarkable; and when she invites me to dinner, she plays on the inflationary use of the word "idea." Nora often seeks to comfort her dialogue partner, and she even has a certain sympathy for Mac(hiavelli). She gives a very convincing explanation for this sympathy, pointing out that Machiavelli at least recognizes his errors and is a passionate man. After I had written to her that her affection was important to Machiavelli, she called me up and told me that she would soon write to me, since she felt pity for Mac, who was now really in a difficult situation so long as he didn't know what she thought of him. Her generosity flags only with regard to Hobbes. She has no time for cynical spitefulness. And yet she tries to understand even him—with great psychological penetration, she sees compensation mechanisms at work in his malice. She has equally strong reservations about the skeptical trio. She maintains a conspicuous distance from Hegel—he is the sole thinker whom she addresses with the formal *Sie,* whereas, with a cheerful lack of inhibition, she addresses the other great thinkers with the informal *Du.* It is notable that she does not agree with Nicholas of Cusa's ideas, but considers them technically interesting.

So far as the content of Nora's letters is concerned, she moves naively through every field of philosophy as if this were a matter of course. For her, however, no problem is a mere academic subject— they are all existentially based, all her questions have to do with the foundation of her personality. The question of God is central—in particular, the question of the compatibility of divine omnipotence and free will concerns her very deeply, along with the problem of the origin of evil. In contrast to her correspondent, whom she contradicts and some of whose questions she does not address, Nora holds fast to her belief in free will, even if her assertions about it are not always consistent, as she herself acknowledges. Her considerations on the doctrine of the Trinity and on Christology are astonishingly precise for a child of eleven or twelve. She has more questions about these doctrines than she would like, but with great intellectual honesty she mentions all the problems that occur to her. Her reflections on the relation between reason and belief, or between moral law and God, as well as on God as the coincidence of opposites, are also noteworthy. Another question on which Nora has earnestly reflected, concerns the issue of whether animals have souls or are like computers, a subject on which she has considerable personal experience. Questions about law and the state constantly come up. Nora is increasingly interested in assessing the value of the modern technological world, and advocates a surprisingly balanced position. She rejects the extreme asceticism of Diogenes, who disapproves of her wish to get a CD-player for Christmas. After my letter of reply, she sent me a package of Gummi-Bears on which she had written: "Gumdrops make children happy—and Diogenes too." Finally, we should note Nora's sensitivity to other cultures as well as to other periods. What she writes about the Renaissance, for example, strikes right to its heart. In general, her historical and literary knowledge and her wide reading should be emphasized.

I have already mentioned that a break is noticeable in the correspondence. At the beginning of 1995 the frequency of the letters decreases; since I usually answered Nora's letters on the day they arrived, this decrease resulted from the fact that Nora henceforth wrote less often. This can be partly explained by increasing academic and other obligations, but the content also changes. The shift in her way of thinking coincides with the beginning of puberty. Nora herself reflects on this in a conversation with her guardian philosopher. Lively imagination subsides; doubt about fundamental convictions spreads. Before she admits that she quarrels with God and even doubts His existence, there are assertions about the soul that deny it an eternal life (because life presupposes corporeality), and affirm only a being of the soul. She is also increasingly troubled by the problem whether there is a Paradise and a Last Judgment.

A few further remarks on how this correspondence was conducted. Nora wrote all her letters very quickly, and completely by herself, usually after she had long thought about the questions involved. A few of them were not even read by her parents. On the other hand, my letters were always read aloud (even if she did not allow anyone else to open them), because Nora could not read my handwriting. (Since I often wrote to her while I was traveling, I could not use a typewriter.) In this context she discussed a few questions with her parents, who gave her certain information; in particular, she constantly consulted lexicons and handbooks to learn about individual philosophers. However, the thoughts and formulations are exclusively hers. Moreover, she always wished to continue the correspondence. She never had to be pressured to write; on the contrary, she reacted with dismay when in the spring of 1995 I suggested that we interrupt our correspondence, since it seemed to be causing her difficulties. Nora had never reckoned with the possibility that these letters might be published. I had repeatedly told her that I had shown her letters to my friends, who had liked them very much, but that was all—I didn't want in any way to endanger their spontaneity. The question of a possible publication of the letters was first discussed with her parents and a few friends. It goes without saying that Nora herself had the last word in making the decision. The break in symmetry represented by this afterword could be repaired by mutual discussion of the meta-level which at first only I had reached, and also by having Nora write her own afterword.

Our letters were scarcely revised for publication; only spelling errors and a few word-repetitions were corrected, a few small passages and personal allusions omitted. It is Nora's wish that her name be kept secret in order to protect her own private sphere. I am grateful to Brigitte Rotzen as well as to Matthias Donath and Dr. Christian Illies, who typed or dictated the letters.

It goes without saying that I do not pretend that the figures I have described here correspond to their historical models. They are ideal types that illustrate certain ideas—I take no responsibility for a possible misunderstanding, namely that I intended to claim that during a train journey the *historical* Kant, Weber, and Heidegger conducted an interesting discussion about ethics and technology.

IV.

Nothing would be more erroneous than to conclude that only a tiny minority of children are capable of writing letters like Nora's. Quite the contrary: questions like those Nora pursues occur to many thoughtful adults, and also to many thoughtful children, and what really requires explanation is not the fact that a child was able to write such letters as the fact that in our culture so few children are able to develop their philosophical curiosity as Nora has. Let's not delude ourselves: our age deals with children's talents as irresponsibly as it deals with scarce natural resources.

In actuality, one thing is clear: even if talent has a genetic basis, the latter is always only a necessary, not a sufficient condition for being able to articulate a talent. This can be shown by recalling that there are ages in which first-class talents spring up all at once, for example in German culture around 1800. Should we assume, for instance, that a few decades earlier something extraordinary happened to the genetic material? This assumption is highly implausible, and it seems far more likely that cultural presuppositions are responsible for the increase in talents. Thus it is obvious, for example, that the state of a discipline's development partly determines what discoveries it can make. After such a spectacular scientific revolution as Newton's, it was a long time before an achievement of comparable originality in physics became possible again. The new paradigm had to be worked out in all its ramifications before a new one became possible, and even a clone of Sir Isaac in the eighteenth century would not have been able to change that, just as conversely a man of comparable heredity in the sixteenth century would not have been able to conceive the *Philosophiae naturalis principia mathematica*. This is valid in large measure for the individual sciences, and an analogous rule holds true for philosophy, and to a lesser extent, for art.

However, in this connection I am not concerned with the pinnacles of achievement, which are never produced by an individual alone, but always by an age as well. People of ordinary gifts also need a certain framework before they can even think of contributing to the further evolution of a field; without such a framework, they cannot develop themselves. Thus talented children must first sense that the effort—always demanding—to develop their own talent is something valuable. Since children's ideas of value always depend on the values recognized in their environments, the importance of the spiritual climate of the family, the circle of friends, the school, the university, and the culture in general must not be underestimated. To begin with the latter, a rigid and authoritarian system that deters innocent questions is lethal to any talent—and a relativistic world-view, which no longer recognizes any qualitative distinctions or objective standards, is equally lethal. It is not hard to see that the latter is the chief danger of our own time. On the other hand, we must cling to these basic insights: (1) developing one's own talent is one of the deepest sources of personal happiness, and everyone has a right to develop his talent so long as doing so does not injure others; (2) everyone benefits from individual talents; and (3) an amazing number of people are talented—in very different ways.

Family relationships can provide a strong counterweight to the spirit of the age. Thus the family in which Nora had the good fortune to grow up also played a role in encouraging her to develop her talent. Having parents who spend a lot of time with their children, the responsibility for a younger sister (the individual's place in a series of siblings is an important determinant of character), the presence of a grandmother who represents the vitality of older traditions, while on the other hand her fragility and greater closeness to death provides a constant reminder of a dimension of human existence that an age oriented toward consumerism and pleasure all too easily represses, and in general, an intellectual atmosphere with many books and only a little television-watching—these sorts of things play a role in the strengthening of talent that is hard to measure but must not be underestimated.

In Nora's private Catholic high school, the personal involvement of the teachers with their students, the institutional connection with supra-personal values, the transmission of humanistic education, and the broad range of activities outside the regular curriculum all make a very positive impression. Her parents had three reasons for choosing this school: first, the fact that Latin was offered as the first foreign language; second, the value system communicated by the school; and third, the interest taken in the students' personalities and talents. It is certainly bad to ask too much of children; but asking too little of them can also lead to disturbing problems—often either to the decay of talents or to the arrogance that springs from frustration. Since children have different talents, a differentiated school system is required.

In fact, there is reason for concern when we examine the contemporary public school system, and the demand for more private schools and universities is in my opinion justified. To be sure, public control over private schools is necessary. But we overestimate the state's possibilities and abilities when we think that it can claim a monopoly on innovative pedagogical or even scholarly ideas. One can no longer support both intellectual pluralism and a state monopoly on education. Naturally, the state should have an interest in encouraging particularly gifted young people. Élites who feel a responsibility for the general welfare are not a danger, they are indispensable in any functional society. Leveling destroys the potential that is urgently needed to solve the increasing problems of industrial societies. Recently there has been much talk about the dim prospects for the human race in the twenty-first century—yet education in general and particularly the encouragement of talents have not yet been transformed in a way adequate to the new demands.

V.

To what extent does philosophy have a special role to play in conceiving a new kind of education as well as in the encouragement of talents? Nora's letters show that philosophy has four different functions in her mental economy: (1) It establishes a relationship between the various areas of knowledge. Questions that emerge in classes in mathematics, English, religion, history, geography, and biology become commensurable in their philosophical dimension. (2) Nora looks to philosophy for answers to questions about morality. (3) Philosophy translates religious convictions into a more rational language. In the course of this attempt at reconstruction, problems and doubts arise, which (4) sharpen her critical consciousness, as she herself recognizes in her reaction to the "Infernal Trio." In fact, these are among philosophy's crucial functions.

To begin with the first, the normal person has a unified consciousness, and he therefore has an absolute need to put into some kind
of order the multiplicity of his experiences and the countless bits
of information that he gathers. However, it is precisely philosophy's
task to determine the place of a given truth in the whole of knowledge. To be sure, the emancipation of the individual sciences from
philosophy was an absolute precondition of their development, and
it also had many beneficial practical aspects. But the freewheeling
that increasingly characterizes the knowledge industry, as well as the
disastrous consequences for our lifeworld of continually expand-
ing specialization, points to the fact that while these emancipatory
tendencies cannot be reversed, they must nevertheless be complemented by a more rigorous reflection on the inner relationship of
knowledge. For example, since human beings are organisms, it is important to understand why and to what extent biological categories
may be useful in comprehending our social behavior and our historical development; however, in determining the relationship as well
as in differentiating the elements of human nature that can be explained biologically, philosophy is necessary. Instruction in philosophy in the schools could therefore help children feel more strongly
the unity of the different disciplines. Conversely, the precision and
also the concreteness of the content would benefit philosophy as well
if philosophical questions were discussed on coming out of classes in
the individual disciplines—and in the latter themselves.

My argument for a larger role for philosophical questioning in
the schools should absolutely not be understood as suggesting that a
special class in philosophy is necessary, even at every level; given the
currently not very cheering state of the discipline, an increase in the
number of positions in philosophy in schools and universities would
not necessarily be beneficial. But the philosophical spirit should have
a place in the schools, and perhaps this will be easier to achieve to
the extent that philosophy does not appear as a separate subject alongside others. It is noteworthy that Hegel, who as rector of a high school
in Nuremberg had more experience with instruction in the schools
than any other great philosopher, was not certain that philosophy
should be a separate subject in the schools. At the request of his
friend Friedrich Immanuel Niethammer, who had been a schools
and church inspector in Munich since 1808 and had written up a neo-
humanistic curriculum for middle schools and high schools in the

kingdom of Bavaria, Hegel wrote on 23 November 1812 a private recommendation regarding "The Presentation of Philosophy in High
Schools" (*Über den Vortrag der Philosophie auf Gymnasien*).[19] In the
letter accompanying it, however, he writes: "One concluding remark
remains to be made, which I did not, however, include, because I am
still of two minds about it—namely, that perhaps all instruction in
philosophy in high schools may seem superfluous, that the study of
the ancients is most suitable for high school students and is, from the
point of view of its substance, the true introduction to philosophy."[20]
Nonetheless, Hegel adds that he finds it hard to argue against his
own subject and his own position, to deprive himself of sustenance,
and then finds an objective argument for instruction in philosophy
after all: the all-too-philological orientation of instruction in the classical languages (which has, of course, increasingly disappeared from
the schools today). All the same, on 16 April 1822, when he was in
Berlin, Hegel wrote another recommendation entitled "On Instruction in Philosophy in High Schools" (*Über den Unterricht in der Philosophie auf Gymnasien*), this time for the Prussian Royal Ministry
for religious, instructional, and medical matters,[21] in which he maintained that the study of the ancients and of the dogmatic content of
Christianity were the best material preparations for the study of philosophy. Hegel strongly rejects the notion that high school instruction in philosophy should concentrate on the history of philosophy—
as was the case for example in Italy, since Giovanni Gentile's edu-
cational reforms. Anticipating the negative consequences of this kind
of instruction, Hegel writes: "However, without presupposing the
speculative idea, it [the history of philosophy] becomes nothing more
than a mere narrative of accidental, idle opinions and easily leads—
and some people are inclined to see this as its goal and an additional
reason for adopting it—to a detrimental, disparaging view of philosophy, and in particular to the idea that with this knowledge everything
becomes mere pointless effort and that for young students it will be a
still more vain effort to spend time on it."[22] Problem-oriented thinking that emerges out of the individual disciplines is surely to be given
precedence over reporting opinions that have no relation to the
child's lifeworld and the other subjects he or she is studying.

Philosophy's second function, which in any case it fulfills for Nora,
has to do with moral orientation—for instance, with regard to the
new demands of the late modernity and the ecological crisis. Moral

questions can never be answered solely by means of descriptive propositions; anyone who knew all that was the case, would still not know how he should behave. To that extent ethics will never be reducible to the other disciplines. Moral education is particularly demanding, because transmitting ethical arguments is far from sufficient—the goal of ethical education has to be to produce moral people, and that is very difficult to achieve unless the ethicist provides a model. Aristotle made fun of any purely theoretical resort to philosophy that corresponds to the behavior of sick people who hang on the physician's every word, but don't follow his recommendations,[23] and Plato, whose concept of education has still not been realized in depth, correctly refers to an art of turning the whole soul in a different direction.[24] However, this sort of education already presupposes the soul; just as it is impossible to implant eyes in a blind person, so the educator cannot create the soul's orientation *ex nihilo,* but only correct it. In fact, it would be presumptuous to maintain that one could make someone moral through education alone—but what good philosophy can do is to overcome the intellectual doubts that rage during adolescence, particularly in gifted children, with regard to the unconditional validity of morality. Nora's character naturally precedes her concern with philosophy—but philosophy can protect this character and help it mature.

In Germany, instruction in ethics is offered as an alternative to religious instruction. This is to be deplored, because a child's religious education should not deprive him or her of access to ethical reflection, and conversely, because it is truly unfortunate when a young person interested in ethics and philosophy has to forego religious instruction. Nora's letters show how closely religious, ethical, and general philosophical questions are interconnected in the child's consciousness. To be sure, a philosophically-based atheism may also be an intellectually and morally respectable position; but an explicit discussion of the question of God's existence and the problem of death is necessary if a young person is not to become an unreflective clod. Making such issues taboo is a crime against the child's soul, which can gain strength to resist if the child knows he can model himself on an authority that transcends actual, socially accepted norms.

However, while every kind of fundamental thinking leads back to God, it is also clear that the philosophical conception of God is not identical with the religious conception. Narrow-minded religious communities may consider that a scandal; for the modern state it is an advantage. In a multicultural, worldwide society we must find common ground beyond not only denominational but also religious differences. The calculations of rational egoisms are too little to maintain a state; appeals to a supposedly revealed text are too much to bind all citizens together. Therefore, as a conversation partner I considered it important to bring other religions and cultures into my letters. I was moved to do so by a dream Nora told me about, and which had troubled her very much: her parents, who have worked to promote Jewish-Christian understanding,[25] were told one evening by a friend, who performs a similar function in a Christian-Islamic association, that many of his Islamic partners hoped there would be a conversation between Christians and Islam. Nora dreamed that Muslims had broken into her house and had tried to convert her to Islam. At first, she asked them to sit down, and offered them tea; then she grew very fearful. In order to calm her fears, I tried to present her with a few possible conversations between religions. In fact, one of the results of intelligent philosophizing that is most important for society consists precisely in learning to engage in unprejudiced conversations with people from other cultures. For then philosophy becomes truly universal.

However, encouragement to engage in philosophy constantly proceeds from children's original questions. Piaget's evolutionism did not prevent him from recognizing that his ideal would be "to remain a child to the end. Childhood is the only real phase of creativity."[26] To cite in conclusion a work that belongs in the philosophical poison cupboard, but which nonetheless constantly emits intellectual illuminations: in his first discourse, Nietzsche's Zarathustra speaks of the three metamorphoses of the spirit. The camel, which bears everything heavy, is succeeded by the lion, whose "I will" is opposed to the great dragon's "thou shalt." However, even the lion is able only to negate, not to create new values. Therefore the predatory lion has to become a child. "The child is innocence and forgetting, a new beginning, a game, a self-propelled wheel, a first movement, a sacred 'Yes' is needed: the spirit now wills his own will, and he who had been lost to the world now conquers his own world."[27] Nietzsche himself did not manage to get beyond the figure of the lion. Perhaps Nora's letters are a model for a future form of philosophy, which will enter into the phase of childhood.

Notes

1. See, for example, H.-L. Freese, *Kinder sind Philosophen* (Weinheim and Berlin, 1989), to which I am indebted for many references.
2. *Zeitschrift für Didaktik der Philosophie* 6 (1984); *Ethik und Sozialwissenschaften* 4 (1993), no. 3:377–438, with a lead article by D. Horster, "Philosophieren mit Kindern," 379–388.
3. *Thinking: The Journal of Philosophy for Children.*
4. *Sophie's World*, trans. Paulette Møller (New York, 1994); original title, *Sofies verden* (Oslo, 1991).
5. Cf. the fine story in Christa Wolf's *Störfall* (Darmstadt and Neuwied, 1987), 105f., in which the child proves to be more philosophical than the scientifically thinking father, and whose questions only the grandmother understands.
6. Cf. Karl Jaspers, *Einführung in die Philosophie* (Munich, 1953), 12: "Children often possess a genius that is lost in adults. It is as if with the passing years we enter into the prison of conventions and opinions, of concealments and unquestioned assumptions, and in so doing lose the child's naturalness."
7. Diogenes Laertius X, 2.
8. Leo Tolstoy, *Childhood, Boyhood, Youth*, trans. Rosemary Edmonds (Harmondsworth and New York, 1964).
9. Ibid., 160 (chap. 20).
10. Ibid., 157 (chap. 19).
11. Ibid., 159.
12. Giambattista Vico, *Opere*, ed. Benedetto Croce and F. Nicolini (2d ed., Bari, 1929), 5:5.
13. *Parerga und Paralipomena*, chap. 28, "*Über Erziehung.*"
14. A classic study by Jean Piaget and Barbel Inhelder is *The Psychology of the Child*, trans. Helen Weaver (New York, 1969). An outstanding introduction to Piaget's work is provided by Th. Kesselring, *Jean Piaget* (Munich, 1988). More critical of Piaget is Margaret C. Donaldson, *Children's Minds* (New York, 1978).
15. Jean Piaget, *The Child's Conception of Time*, trans. A. J. Pomerans (New York, 1971).
16. Giovanni Pascoli writes in his famous essay "Il fanciullino": "O, child, who can only think in your own way, in a childlike way, which is deeply, because it moves us all at once, without making us descend down the levels of thought one after another, into the abyss of truth . . ." *Opere*, ed. M. Perugi (Milan and Naples, 1981), 2:1650.
17. 4th ed., Göttingen, 1967. The same holds for the "subject indexes" in the four volumes of the *Handbook of Child Psychology*, ed.

P. H. Mussen (4th ed., New York, 1983). However, there are long articles on "Logical Reasoning" (by M. D. S. Braine and B. Rumain, 3:263–340) and on "Morality" (by J. R. Rest, 3:556–629) that have implications for children's philosophical thought. It would be interesting to investigate when children are able to understand the questions whether everything is not merely a dream, whether God is responsible for evil, and so on—that is, the questions that Nora discusses in such a lively fashion.

18. Cf. Matthew Lipman, *Pixie* (Montclair, NJ, 1981), as well as Matthew Lipman and Ann Margaret Sharp, *Looking for Meaning: Instructional Manual to Accompany Pixie* (Montclair, NJ, 1982); Gareth B. Matthews, *Dialogues with Children* (Cambridge, MA, 1984) and *Philosophy of Childhood* (Cambridge, MA, 1994). A useful collection is M. Lipman and A. M. Sharp, *Growing Up with Philosophy* (Philadelphia, 1978).

19. G. W. F. Hegel, *Werke in zwanzig Bänden* (Frankfurt, 1969–1971), 4:403–416.

20. *Briefe von und an Hegel*, 4 vols., ed. J. Hoffmeister (3rd ed., Hamburg, 1969–1981), 1:418 f. Cf. also Hegel's letter of 24 March 1812 to Niethammer: "But too much philosophy is probably already taught in high schools; it can justifiably be foregone at the lower levels." (1:397)

21. *Werke*, 9:31–41.

22. Ibid., 9:36.

23. *Nicomachean Ethics* 1105b 12ff.

24. *Politics* 518b ff.

25. Nora's familiarity with Judaism is shown by her allusion to Martin Buber, *Die chassidischen Bücher* (Hellerau, 1928), 532 f., in her letter of 27 October 1994.

26. J.-C. Bringuier, *Conversations libres avec Jean Piaget* (Paris, 1977), 170.

27. *Thus Spoke Zarathustra*, in *The Portable Nietzsche*, ed. and trans. Walter Kaufmann (New York, 1954), 139.

Finally

by Nora K.

Dear Reader,

I would like to add a few concluding words to our correspondence. But it's hard, because I don't know what to say.

What should one say to someone whom one doesn't know and who could be anyone?

However, I'll try. To do so I have to remember the time three years ago, which again is not easy, because many things have changed, in me as well.

It will be best to begin with the evening when I met Vittorio. Mama had, I think, participated in a conference on a philosophical subject, where she had met him, among other people. On leaving, she invited Vittorio to visit us sometime. And so I got to know him, and I still recall how he came up to me beaming, his head tilted a little to one side, as he always does when he greets someone, and we shook hands.

A short time later, he came to visit us again, and we all sat around the supper table and ate pizza. Vittorio learned that I was reading "Sophie's World," and told me that whenever I had questions, I could call him up. But I didn't call him; instead, he called me, after Mama told him about the Dino-problem. We talked about it, and he explained it to me as well as he could. Soon afterward, I was given a marzipan dinosaur—it became the motto of our correspondence: Vittorio was called "Idea" and I "Dino-Nora." How mysterious it was when I received the first philosophical letter, just like my "friend" Sophie. Only I could answer, and Sophie couldn't.

And so we began to write to each other (and we still do).

I didn't know anything about a possible publication; it was only just before I wrote my last letter printed here that I heard about the plans. Naturally, I found the idea great at first, but then I had to think about it for a long time. Sometimes I was on the point of saying no, because after all they were *our* letters! What would other people want with them? Why should I expose all my thoughts? So that somebody else could draw some kind of scientific conclusions from them? No, I was not yet ready for that!

But then it occurred to me that our letters might give other people, especially children, encouragement and pleasure, so that they might take an interest in our world and its wonders, and strengthen their resistance to indifference and heartlessness about the future. I don't know whether we have succeeded in doing that, but I hope we have.

On the table next to me stands a little dinosaur with the inscription: "A nice guy"! . . .

Index of Names

CPSIA information can be obtained
at www.ICGtesting.com
Printed in the USA
BVHW031335190619
551429BV00003B/6/P